AHEAD OF THE CURVE

Amber C. Saunders

About Peterson's

Peterson's provides the accurate, dependable, high-quality education content and guidance you need to succeed. No matter where you are on your academic or professional path, you can rely on Peterson's print and digital publications for the most up-to-date education exploration data, expert test-prep tools, and top-notch career success resources—everything you need to achieve your goals.

For more information, contact Peterson's, 3 Columbia Circle, Suite 205, Albany, NY 12203; 800-338-3282 Ext. 54229; or find us online at www.petersonsbooks.com.

ISBN: 978-0-7689-3871-5

Printed in the United States of America

10 9 8 7 6 5 4 3 2 1   16 15 14

First Edition

This book is dedicated to my family:

The Sims, Saunders, Jeffress, and Dyett clans.
Look at what you guys made!

And to the best grandmothers on earth:
Dorothea Cecile Rowling, Alice Cecile Dyett, and Rosa Lee Saunders

Acknowledgments

Mom, thank you isn't enough and nothing I say can even come close. You've moved mountains for me. Thank you.

Dad, I don't know how you snap me back to reality, but you always do. Thanks for keeping me calm through it all.

I have a ton of people to thank. I hope I don't forget a single soul. If I did, I'll thank you in person:

Felecia Hatcher (if it wasn't for you!), Donald L. Bedney, III, Anthony Flynn, Kristen Daniel, Darrell Glasco (my fairy godfather), Hashim Bello (I miss you), Sheryl Harrison (you are going to heaven), Michele Butts, Frederick Owens, Nicole Heeder, Rachel Sanders-Hurley), Emily Lofthouse, Luisa Rosas, Lavonne Caesar, Radiah Fowler, Luke Riggins, Magnus Greaves, Phil Rugile, 100 Urban Entrepreneurs, Suresh May, Quinetha Frasier, Brian "The Dreamer" Johnson, Rishal Stanciel, Kristin Grier, Sabrina Willis, Jacque Thornton, Javier Thompson, Quinn and Andrew Taylor, Mrs. Reid (You will always be my Mrs. Reid. I can't say your first name. It just feels wrong.), Ms. Harris (same goes for you Ms. Harris), Principal Lamb (you'll always be my principal), and anyone else who has had to deal with me during the time I was writing this book or in life. You've been through a lot. God Bless You.

I have never given birth, but I finally understand the importance of midwives. Writing a book is hard, and that is probably an understatement. Dealing with someone who has written or is writing a book is probably much more difficult. I've had amazing people help me get this book out. They actually made me sound lucid, so I am eternally grateful. Thank you Bernadette Webster, Stephanie Benyo, Ovetta Sampson, and the women who got their hands dirty, Kathy Holley and Jill Schwartz.

Contents

CONTENTS

CONTENTS

CONTENTS

Introduction

High school graduates heading off to college face some startling statistics. The good news is that 66 percent of the nation's high school seniors were enrolled in a college or university the October after they graduated high school. The bad news is that about 7 percent of high school students drop out before they even get to their senior year. This tells a concerned parent that the journey to college starts long before a teenager picks out a senior prom dress or tuxedo.

Yet, many students wait until their junior and senior years to begin thinking about college readiness. This is a grave mistake. The skills a student needs to do well on college admission exams must be cultivated throughout a student's high school career. For example, here's how the College Board, the governing body that produces the SAT college entrance exam, offers students a head start. In 2011, it rolled out "ReadiStep," an $8 exam given to eighth graders to assess their college readiness. Yes, that's right—eighth grade!

By the time students reach high school, they may already be behind the curve. But this book can help them catch up. The information here will help you get your child *ahead of the college readiness curve* and firmly on the path to college.

This book is designed to help the proactive parent. You need this book if:

- You haven't heard any discussion about college-prep testing or college-prep classes at your child's elementary or middle school. Such talk is the norm at most private schools with a college-preparatory curriculum.

- You cannot afford to send your child to a private, college-prep high school with a robust college-track curriculum.

- Your child is the first one in your family heading to college
- You went to college, but so much has changed since then, and you need help understanding what today's high school student needs to get in.

This book will provide simple, yet strategic, steps to inform and empower you to take control of your child's academic career. These steps will help ensure your child is prepared to conquer the barriers that keep many students from graduating high school and realizing their collegiate dreams. Use this book as a road map through your child's high school years and ultimately as a guide to your student's successful college entry.

Why I Wrote This Book

As a college graduate and attorney, I've taken many standardized tests in my life, from the Preliminary SAT (PSAT) to the Georgia Bar Examination. My fascination with testing and test preparation began my senior year of high school when I bombed the ACT®. I was completely traumatized by my score. I vowed to improve. Yet my mother and I didn't have the money for a test-preparation course, and my school did not provide such resources. My mother didn't take the ACT when she was in high school, so she couldn't help me prepare. I was on my own.

I purchased two ACT test-prep books and went to work. I worked through the books each day after school and took practice exams on the weekends leading up to the next test date. When I retook the test, my score increased significantly. I was admitted to college and awarded several scholarships. It didn't hit me until later, when I prepared for the Law School Admission Test (LSAT®), that I had a revelation. Performing well on standardized tests has less to do with your intellect and more to do with your test-taking competency. With this knowledge I have honed my test-taking abilities and have taught many students to conquer standardized exams, much as I did. These test-taking strategies led me to start a tutoring company, Enrichment Prep.

Founded in 2009, Enrichment Prep prepared students for the various college-prep standardized tests including the PSAT/NMSQT®, SAT®, and ACT®. In addition to teaching students test-taking strategies, parents I spoke to also wanted to learn other ways to prepare their children for college. While tutoring students, dozens of parents asked me the same questions about creating a college-prep pathway for their children.

This book answers those questions and was created as a resource for frustrated and discouraged parents whose schools do not have the resources to adequately prepare their children for college-preparatory success. In this book, you will learn the following:

- How to direct your child's academic career toward a college track
- How to select the right courses to put your child on the path to college
- How to make smart, informed test-preparation choices that will save you money and time
- How to become an asset to your child's collegiate aspirations

The chapters in this book are organized by grade.

Chapter 1–Ninth Grade: The Journey Begins walks you through your child's ninth-grade year. Whether your student is starting high school or is still in middle school, this grade is an important one on the road to college. This chapter will offer such advice as how to interact with your child's guidance counselor, how to help your student create their college-prep schedule, and what to do when there aren't many options available at your student's school. You'll also find some helpful information on college majors and why it isn't too early to begin this discussion with your child, along with advice on helping your student start their academic résumé. By the end of this chapter, I hope you will feel better equipped to help your child navigate what can be a very tumultuous time in his or her life.

Chapter 2–Tenth Grade: Preparing Now Pays Off Later covers the tenth-grade year. The tenth grade is all about helping your child maintain good grades, continuing the college major discussion, keeping your student's guidance counselor in the loop, getting your student ready to take the first of those necessary standardized college admission tests, and discovering who your child is—academically, socially, and civically.

Chapter 3–Junior Year: Important Decisions Ahead focuses on test preparation and narrowing down your student's college list. We'll help you wrap your mind around the numerous standardized tests your student will face, from the PSAT/NMSQT to the SAT and ACT, and we'll discuss the advantages of your student taking an early administration of the ACT and SAT to see where he or she stands. We also discuss college visits and how to help your student determine the colleges and universities that are (hopefully) the best fit.

With a drum roll, we dive into **Chapter 4–Senior Year: It All Comes Down to This!** This chapter is extensive. We go through the senior year schedule, college applications, recommendation letters, and more. By the end, you will be a pro.

We even have something for those parents who don't have time to read the entire book. In **Chapter 5–The Path to College: List by List,** you'll find checklists and a list of To Dos for parents who just need to make sure they have covered all their bases—no definitions and no explanations, only action items.

For the nitty-gritty on how to pay for your student's college education, we've compiled lots of helpful information in **Chapter 6—Financial Fundamentals: Planning and Paying for College.** Here you'll find details on saving for college, the financial aid process (FAFSA, the CSS/Financial Aid PROFILE®), financial aid award letters, and types of aid—grants, loans, federal aid, state aid, and scholarships.

Chapter 7–Summer: An Important Part of Your Student's College Plan offers great information and advice on how to turn summer vacations into meaningful, well-spent days, weeks, and months.

Finally, I hope you'll find that the **Appendix: Resources** offers you helpful information, with links to relevant organizations, businesses, federal programs, and more. There's a lot of information available online, but these listed resources are a great starting point to help you learn about financial fundamentals, getting organized, majors and careers, standardized testing and test-prep information, summer programs, and supplemental learning programs.

If there is a topic you think should be added, feel free to send me your suggestions or questions. I'd love to hear from you. Contact me at skydiver@enrichmentprep.com with questions or concerns.

Now, let's get started!

CHAPTER 1

Ninth Grade:
The Journey Begins

CHAPTER 1

What do you remember about your freshman year of high school? Was it difficult for you? It was for me. Not because the kids were mean (which they were) or because classes were hard (which they were). It was difficult because I had no idea what in the world I was doing.

I thought I'd had it made in middle school. I was so happy in the eighth grade and was excited to graduate and move on to ninth grade, which was in high school. Then, suddenly, I had to start from scratch to find my place in the high school environment. Oh, the pressure.

Hopefully, it's not that dramatic for your child, but I'm guessing it might be. On top of all that, this chapter will tell you that it's time for your child to get serious about preparing for college and thinking about majors—but you are there to help with that process. I want you to help your child understand that the next four years are going to lay the groundwork for his or her college success. At the same time, I want you to be mindful of how difficult this year could potentially be for your child. We walk a fine line, but we must still walk.

My hope is that by the end of this chapter:

- You will be friendly with the school guidance counselor, or at minimum have a new level of respect for the job.
- You will be able to create your own college-prep schedule for your student.
- You will know the significance of your state's graduation requirements.
- You will know the difference between the various high school diploma categories.

- You will know what kind of courses to look for at your student's school and elsewhere.
- You will understand the pros and cons of AP, I.B., and dual enrollment courses.
- You will know how to find outside options if there aren't many course selections at your child's school.
- You will begin brainstorming with your child about a college major.
- You will start getting your feet wet with college planning.

As you go through this book, keep in mind that no two high schools are the same. Even the term "high school" means different things in different communities—some high schools are grades 9 through 12, while others are grades 10 through 12. Some schools use a traditional seven- or eight-period class day; others have block scheduling. Some use different terminology or have unique programs that may not be well publicized. That's why it's important for you to be informed, involved, and aware of the opportunities available to your student!

And while we'll use the term "college" throughout this book, "college" doesn't necessarily mean four years on a traditional campus. What it means is *higher education,* whether it's a college or university, a technical school, a junior or community college, an online degree program, or something else. The world of higher education is changing and expanding all the time. What is important is that you and your student recognize that it's a necessary and valuable next step after high school, and it's a step that you want to take.

Let's begin!

Get to Know Your Student's Guidance Counselor

One of the biggest resources you will have during your child's matriculation through high school is his or her guidance counselor. I've seen guidance counselors perform miracles. My high school counselor, Ms. Harris, did just that when one of my classmates didn't have enough language arts credits to graduate on time. Ms. Harris signed her up for a correspondence course the very semester we were scheduled to graduate. My classmate rocked the course and walked with us in cap and gown.

Now I'm not encouraging you to expect miracles. That's simply not fair. What you can expect is something more attainable and that's *collaboration—working together.*

When I speak of *working together,* I'm speaking of equipping yourself with the right information so that you and your child can work with the guidance counselor to use the best resources at your disposal. To do so, you must understand what questions to ask, when to ask them, and the best way to go about asking the right questions.

When you start asking is important, and it's tricky. It's tricky for several reasons. Some schools do not assign counselors to students until the school year begins. In addition, many schools don't release students' schedules until a few weeks before school starts, and some only distribute schedules on the first day of school. If that's the case, you may want to reach out to another contact or administrator at the school to get the information you need. If you try to set the appointment during the planning period, you may have a hard time getting a response. If you wait until the semester has already started, it may be difficult for you to make necessary changes in your child's schedule.

Questions that aren't related to your child's schedule can be asked of any counselor at the school, so you don't have to wait until his or her counselor is assigned. If you are trying to find out what your high school's graduation rate is, *when* you ask that question is extremely important. Ideally, this is the kind of question you should ask when your child is in eighth grade so that if you learn that your child's potential high school isn't producing graduates at an acceptable rate, you'll have the time you need to research other schools and find one that does. If you live in a district with school choice, you should have time to ask the necessary questions to be able to make an informed decision about where your student goes to high school.

It's important to keep some things in mind during this process of working with your student's guidance counselor. First and foremost, as the saying goes, "the squeaky wheel gets the grease." Your child will get more attention, assistance, and exposure to more opportunities if you make it known that you need some help. That doesn't mean that you should call every day or even once a week, but you should keep in reasonable contact with your child's guidance counselor. A counselor who knows your student and his or her interests well enough is likely to remember to send an e-mail or give you a quick call if an interesting opportunity arises.

In addition, different schools have different types of counselors. Your school may have a general counselor who provides academic and emotional guidance; other schools may have counselors on staff who help guide students' college selection process or who provide psychological support. In order for your counselor to be a good resource to you and your child, you need to know what his or her role is at the school, so you are reaching out for the right information or assistance.

Finally, how do you start? Call your child's assigned guidance counselor and schedule a face-to-face appointment—and keep that appointment. That means that you need to come to the appointment prepared, with real questions that can give you both answers and actions that you can take.

Asking the Right Questions

Following are some suggested questions to get the ball rolling. We'll go through each question and break down why you ask it, what it means, and what steps you can take with each answer you receive.

What percentage of your school's students graduates from high school?

There are several factors that determine whether a student graduates from high school. Still, graduation rates can serve as an important way to gauge accountability for your high school. High school graduation—once the end of educational achievement for many—is now really just the starting line. The changing economy means that people who don't receive any postsecondary education may have access to only 40 percent of the jobs in the next decade.

The good news is that graduation rates are actually on the rise in the United States. As a result, the nation is on track to achieve a 90 percent national graduation rate by the class of 2020. The graduation rate—from which you can also determine the dropout rate—will tell you something about the school. The general conclusion to draw from a graduation rate of 60 percent or lower is that the school is considered low performing.

What percentage of your school's students attends college upon graduation?

If your child's school has a solid graduation rate, that's great! Then the next question is this: how many of those who graduate go on to attend a college or university? If the graduates aren't attending college, you need to know why. It may be that students in your area are going into technical professions rather than attending a university. Or it could be because the students aren't scoring high enough on standardized tests and, as a result, are going to community colleges before moving on to four-year institutions. This statistic could be a good indication of whether the school is equipping students with the skills they need to be attractive to colleges.

What are the average scores on the ACT, SAT, and PSAT/NMSQT at the school?

It's debatable whether standardized test results correlate to the ability to perform well in college. I know some students who are great test-takers but fall short at completing in-class or homework assignments. Nevertheless, the fact remains that your child is going to have to take those tests in order to gain admission to a college or university. For that reason, you should know if your child's school is producing high school graduates who consistently perform well on these tests. Low scores may indicate that the school's academic program is not rigorous enough. The results can also indicate that the students at the school aren't exposed to these tests early enough or haven't prepared. You need to know the results and determine what your school's track record is in this area in order to put your child in the best position possible to achieve success.

On average, are there any test problem subjects for students at the school?

Patterns matter. I vividly remember a school I coached at where students had a huge problem with math. Students took the ACT, and *every single student* scored significantly lower in math than the national average. What's even more unbelievable is that the school failed to see the pattern or do anything about it. At that point, in my opinion, it is not the students' fault. That is a school problem or a math teacher problem, and it needed to be addressed. It's not something a test-prep company or teacher should be brought in to correct. These students needed significant remediation in math.

A lot of the parents I spoke with at the school weren't in a position to send their children to a different school and felt discouraged by the low test scores. I encouraged them to look at it from a different perspective. Imagine what position they would have been in if they had not been aware of the scores. Now, they KNOW where the weaknesses are going to show up. This can be handled—whether via a math tutor, regular supplementary lessons built into the child's homework sessions, or staying after school with the math teacher to get additional help—there are things that can be done!

You want to know your school's strengths and weaknesses. If there are weaknesses, don't be discouraged. Knowledge is power—and that's not just a cliché. If you know what you are facing, you can plan ways to compensate for the potential deficiency. You can monitor your student's progress in the subject. You can find tutors or subject-based programs for your student to participate in during the summer. All is not lost. But if you don't know where your school or your student stands, you are left defenseless during application time when your student needs strong scores.

Does the school offer the ACT Plan and Explore in addition to the PSAT/NMSQT to students in grades 9 and 10?

The earlier your student is exposed to college entrance standardized tests the better. Explore is the eighth- and ninth-grade version of the ACT, and Plan is the tenth-grade version. Both test the information your student should know by each grade. They provide a great preview of the ACT format for your student. By the eleventh grade, your student should be practicing with the real ACT.

The PSAT/NMSQT is the precursor to the SAT. Students take the official PSAT/NMSQT in October of their junior year. Some schools allow students to take the test during their tenth-grade year, but it doesn't count toward consideration for the National Merit scholarship until junior year. I have heard of some schools providing practice versions of the PSAT/NMSQT as early as eighth grade.

If your school doesn't administer these tests during ninth or tenth grade, you can purchase copies of the test on your own or have your student take practice versions of the test online. We will discuss test prep in depth later in the chapter on eleventh grade. However, if you want to start early, great! Take a sneak peak. You will also find test-prep options in the Resource List in the Appendix of this book.

Can the counselor provide you with a copy of your child's proposed ninth-grade course schedule?

As mentioned before, it would be ideal if you can get this question answered during the second semester of your student's eighth grade year. Even if you are only able to get a sample schedule, it can help you prepare for the upcoming year.

Once you have your child's schedule, compare it to the general college-prep diploma schedule. Are there any deviations from the general schedule? If so, why are they putting your child in a different course? At the end of each school year, ask for the schedule for the upcoming semester to ensure that your student stays on track. Asking for this schedule early gives you a chance to intervene when you see your child's schedule isn't sticking to the plan.

If you have to wait until a couple of weeks before school starts to get your child's schedule, don't fret. Most schools have an Add/Drop period before the course schedule becomes final. If, for example, your son is having a problem with a class or two on his schedule, you'll want to stay on top of things to be sure that he is working with his guidance counselor to modify his schedule prior to the deadline date.

Does the school offer academic support programs for struggling students and in what subjects?

Ask this question to determine what resources are available at your school, free or otherwise. This helps you create an affordable strategy if/when your student is struggling in a particular subject. These resources can bolster your student's knowledge in a subject in which he or she already has a solid foundation. This book contains a list of numerous outside resources, but nothing beats local and easily accessible resources that are available in your community. You can never have too many resources at your disposal.

Does the school offer general, vocational or tech-prep, and college-prep diplomas?

A general diploma, a vocational or tech-prep diploma, and a college-prep diploma have different requirements. A **general education diploma** is generally obtained by following a curriculum of basic, fundamental courses and maintaining the minimum GPA requirement. This track is generally ideal for a student who wants a high school diploma but doesn't intend to attend college.

A **vocational or tech-prep diploma** allows a student to take courses that relate to a particular trade or vocation. This diploma locks the student into a particular vocational track, based on the trade he or she chooses. These diplomas prepare students for careers directly out of high school.

A **college-prep diploma** requires the student to complete a certain mandated curriculum in order to prepare for college upon graduation from high school. The curriculum generally requires additional credits for core subjects such as English, math, science, and foreign language (referred to as world, modern, or global language at some schools).

Can the counselor provide you with a copy of your school's graduation requirements for a college-prep diploma?

Since you are reading this book, I assume that you want your child to graduate with a college-prep diploma if it is available at your school. Now, you need to see how that diploma's requirements compare to your state's graduation requirements in order to be certain that the diploma requirements meet or exceed the state requirements and to see if there is room within the diploma requirements to add other advanced courses.

Can the counselor provide you with a copy of a sample college-prep academic course schedule?

You need a copy of this schedule to compare and/or make additions when drafting your child's high school schedule. Having this schedule handy can help keep your child on track each year to graduate with a college-prep diploma.

Does the school offer Advanced Placement (AP®) or International Baccalaureate (I.B.) courses?

Advanced Placement (AP) courses were created by the College Board to offer college-level curriculum to high school students. Many colleges and universities provide course credit to students who earn a particular score on an AP exam in that subject. That's the benefit of taking these classes in high school. It's often a win-win situation: students prepare for college-level school work, and, if they score high enough, they earn college credit. The biggest benefit may be the possibility of your student skipping entry-level courses (which equates to less tuition in the long run).

The **International Baccalaureate (I.B.) Diploma Programme** is a two-year internationally accepted college-preparatory curriculum; however students at I.B. schools can also choose to take individual I.B. courses and earn college credit, depending on how well they score on the exam for those courses.

If your school offers AP and I.B. courses, when the time comes, you should weigh the benefits against the potential barriers to success. The assignments are very time consuming, and they require self-discipline. If your daughter is playing basketball and doesn't get home to start homework until 9 p.m., you won't have a happy student when she has to wake up at 6 a.m. and is sleepy during classes from staying up until the wee hours studying. AP and I.B. courses have to make sense for your child's schedule, temperament, and abilities. We will discuss AP and I.B. courses in further detail a little later in this chapter.

What courses does the counselor recommend for a college-bound student?

Your high school counselor is one of your most valuable resources. Your counselor knows the best (and required) courses for your student to take. Your counselor is likely familiar with the faculty members and their teaching styles and can recommend instructors whose teaching styles best suit your child (although this may not be possible in large high schools).

What are the prerequisite courses for the college-prep schedule, and is there a minimum GPA requirement for those courses?

Most upper-level courses require that a student complete certain prerequisite courses prior to being eligible to enroll. If you plan to enroll your student in one of those courses, you should encourage him or her to take the prerequisite and get the grades necessary to qualify for the upper-level courses.

Does the counselor recommend any local summer programming for a college-bound student?

Your counselor can be your key to success in finding great summer programs. Yes, you can do the research and find great programs on your own. However, keep in mind that the majority of the valuable opportunities for students at your school probably pass through the hands of your guidance counselor. If your counselor knows your student's interests and goals, he or she can let you and your student know about any summer programs, community service opportunities, or courses that might be a perfect fit.

Course Planning

In high school, I found it extremely annoying and embarrassing that my lovely mother was always at my school. Every teacher, principal, guidance counselor, staff member, and janitor knew my mother by name. She spoke with every teacher and made appointments with my guidance counselor every semester. She reviewed and approved my course schedule every semester before I was able to register for class. Can you imagine? I was mortified. In hindsight, however, my mother's influence was the key to my academic success. When I had issues in class, my mother knew before the bus dropped me off at home because she built relationships with the people who opened the door to a successful high school career. Aleta Saunders held the embarrassing key. You can be the key to your child's college dreams. I am excited to help you create a college-prep schedule that helps your student along his or her path to college.

In this section, you will learn about basic graduation requirements, what academic subjects are essential for each of the four years your child is in high school, as well as how to create a college-preparatory course schedule to ensure your child meets and exceeds college entrance requirements. If you weren't pleased with some of the answers you received in the previous section, don't fret. All is not lost. I will show you how to use the resources you have at your child's current school, how to shore up weak areas by choosing appropriate summer-enhancement programs, and finally, how you may want to use tutoring and online programs to make sure your child has everything he or she needs to create a solid college-bound academic path.

State Graduation Requirements

Before you can get into the fun of selecting courses with your student, you have to take care of the basics. These are the required courses in core subjects that every student must take, and successfully master, in order to graduate from high school. Usually, students are automatically enrolled in these basic courses by the school registrar, but every school is different, so make sure. It would be wise to take part in the course selection process with your child. I believe this is too important for your child to do solo.

While course selection may vary from school to school, it is very likely every school has a registrar and/or counselors. You should speak to both counselors and registrars and get recommendations. Cross-check the courses available at your student's school with the graduation requirements of your state. For example, here is a list of graduation requirements for the state for Georgia for 2014. Use this as a reference only because your state may differ.

Current GEORGIA Graduation Requirements	
English/Language Arts	4
Math	4
Science	4
Social Studies	3
Physical Education	½
Health	½
Required Electives	4
(Career, technical, and agricultural education, and/or foreign language/Latin, and/or fine arts)	
TOTAL UNITS	**23**

In this example, one unit is an entire academic year of class. One unit equates to 120 in-class hours of education in that particular course. If your school is on a semester schedule, then you will likely see that the courses offered each semester are half of a unit. Know which courses your student needs to take every quarter and/

or semester. Once you have the basics mapped out, move on to additional courses.

Beyond the Basics

The goal in being hands-on in creating your child's schedule is to ensure that your child is able to rise to the challenge of college and its rigorous course load. Studies have shown that more than half of the students graduating from high school are below college-readiness benchmarks in at least one of the core subjects. The assumption to be drawn from this is that if students aren't scoring high enough on the college-readiness benchmarks on the ACT or SAT, then they probably won't be able to succeed in a college class in those subjects either.

When looking at a student's transcripts, colleges need to see that your student has mastered the basic content knowledge necessary to provide a foundation for entry-level college courses. The skills your child has developed, beyond the basic content knowledge, will factor into whether he or she will be successful in the course. Your son or daughter builds those skills in tough courses. Letting your child take the "easy A" classes may help build a high GPA, but it won't prepare him or her for college.

So how do college-bound students develop these college-readiness skills if they're not part of their basic academic courses? Welcome to the college-track course schedule.

This selection of courses should include: college-prep classes, AP or I.B. classes, and/or dual-enrollment classes (actual college classes students take while still in high school). You also want to be aware of, and regularly reference, the electives available at your high school.

Elective Courses

Electives are courses that count toward your student's diploma, but aren't directly a part of the core curriculum. Electives give your student the opportunity to explore his or her interests, prepare for college, and prepare for the job market. Studies have shown that students are likely to choose a major or career that correlates with a course they took as an elective in high school.

If your child plans to attend a technical college, this is a good opportunity to explore those subjects in an elective course. From the budding chef to the future engineer, a student can get her first taste of these careers in elective courses.

In addition, the electives that your child chooses can give employers and college admissions officers a way to learn more about your child, their interests, and their career goals.

Your student can also benefit from mixing it up a bit with course selection, including both academic and practical elective courses. For example, schools often offer life skills courses such as financial management, which can teach invaluable skills for inexperienced college-bound teenagers getting their first taste of the real world.

College-Prep Classes

A college-prep course is a course that meets the more stringent scholastic requirements for entry into colleges and universities. These courses provide the foundation students need to survive a college course load. Students taking college-preparatory courses *should* have an increased quantity of homework, and expectations to achieve are at a higher level to ready them for the intensity of the college academic environment.

Advanced Placement (AP) Classes

The next step beyond college-prep courses is Advanced Placement or AP courses. AP is a national program created by The College Board that offers college-level curriculum and examinations to high school students. In many schools, students can enroll in AP courses if they successfully complete prerequisite courses and/or achieve a certain grade point average. A panel of experts and college-level educators in each subject create the AP curriculum. To receive the

AP designation, the course must be audited by the College Board to determine whether it satisfies the AP curriculum requirements. One of the benefits of the AP curriculum is that it should, in theory, provide AP students in one school with the same rigor provided to other AP students taking the same course all over the country.

Simply taking the course doesn't get your student into college. As with most things academic, your student must take an exam for each AP course and score at a certain level in order to have those courses potentially recognized by the college of his or her choosing. Although there is a cost for each AP exam taken, by successfully completing the course and scoring high enough on the exam, your student can potentially save on college tuition, fees, and textbook costs.

Currently, more than 90 percent of colleges and universities throughout the United States offer college credit and/or the ability to place out of an introductory course for qualifying AP exam scores, but minimum requirements vary by school. For example, one college might accept a score of 3 while another will only accept a score of 4 or 5.

There are currently 34 courses and exams available through the AP Program. Here is a complete list of the courses available, effective 2014:

Art History
Biology
Calculus AB
Calculus BC
Chemistry
Chinese Language and
    Culture
Computer Science A
English Language and
    Composition
English Literature and
    Composition
Environmental Science
European History
French Language
German Language
Government and
    Politics: Comparative
Government and
    Politics: United States
Human Geography
Italian Language and
    Culture
Japanese Language
    and Culture
Latin: Vergil

Macroeconomics	Spanish Language
Microeconomics	Spanish Literature
Music Theory	Statistics
Physics B	Studio Art: 2-D Design
Physics C: Electricity and Magnetism	Studio Art: 3-D Design
	Studio Art: Drawing
Physics C: Mechanics	United States History
Psychology	World History

For more information, you may want to visit https://apstudent. collegeboard.org/exploreap.

Your student does *not* need to take a ton of AP courses to be ready for college. But you do need to feel secure that the courses at your student's high school have a certain level of rigor in order to both ease your student's transition into college and prepare them for the course work there. Throughout the high school years, pay attention to how much work your student is actually bringing home. That can indicate if your child is being challenged appropriately or if he or she should be taking more challenging classes.

International Baccalaureate (I.B.)

Some schools may offer the International Baccalaureate Programme instead of AP classes. The I.B. Diploma Programme covers two years with a full schedule of challenging courses and other requirements (an extended essay, community service, physical activity, and artistic expression) designed to develop critical-thinking skills and provide the student with a comprehensive global education (I.B. courses and requirements are the same worldwide; students' work is often evaluated by instructors in other countries). Students may choose to undertake the Full Diploma, or they can take individual classes, similar to the AP process. Students must take an exam in each course they take, and achieving a particular score on those exams can earn students college credits.

For additional information, you might want to check out this site: http://www.ibo.org/.

Dual Enrollment

Dual enrollment is when a high school student is earning both high school and college credits at the same time. It may be an option if you want your child to get accustomed to more rigorous work than your high school currently offers. You should discuss this possibility with your student's guidance counselor; this may not be available at all schools. In addition, you need to find out whether the colleges your child plans to apply to will accept those credits. If your school doesn't offer many AP courses, this may be a good option to even the playing field for your student during the application process.

If AP, I.B., and Dual Enrollment Aren't an Option

There is no one way to educate a child. Your priority is to see that your child learns and thrives in both academic and nonacademic environments. That means, if AP or I.B. courses aren't offered at your school and if dual enrollment isn't an option, your child still needs to develop the skills needed to excel in college. Your child can consult a tutor, take classes at the local library, and enroll in online courses. As previously mentioned, you also need to refer to the electives available at your child's schools.

Tips to Selecting the Right Course

There are thousands of resources online and off-line for your student. If, for example, your student needs to find a course that isn't available at his or her high school, there are a few things to keep in mind before diving in.

First, where do you find these courses? The first person you should reach out to for an answer to this question is your guidance counselor. When my former company, Enrichment Prep, wanted to offer services to high school students, the first group we spoke to was guidance counselors. When The Gifted Education Foundation, a national nonprofit seeking to create a marketplace of leaders of first-generation college graduates, is looking for high school students to enroll in its enrichment program, requests are sent to guidance counselors. So take my advice, and send a quick e-mail to your student's guidance counselor for a few suggestions. I guarantee you won't regret it.

You can also look to your local library. In Atlanta, where I live, there are several libraries that offer college-prep and GED® Test courses (through third-party providers, of course). Many libraries offer SAT/ACT prep as well as tutoring services. Visit the library in your area and request a list of services and courses it offers.

Although searching online can be overwhelming, it's certainly a great way to discover additional resource options. Just be careful—simply because a company or program pops up at the top of your Google search, it doesn't mean that it will be the best option for your child. Make sure you check out any test-prep company to make sure its claims are legitimate, and, of course, make sure the cost fits within your budget. To help you out a bit, I've put together a list of some recommended options. You'll find the list in the **Appendix: Resources** section at the back of this book.

In addition, you need to find out whether the course credit will be accepted by your high school. If your child wants to take a course at the local community college, check with his or her guidance counselor to verify the credits can transfer successfully. If a course is offered online, make sure it's offered by an accredited* institution, and, again, check with your student's school to be certain that the credits can count toward your student's diploma. It's likely the guidance counselor or school administrator will need to evaluate the course description and syllabus, among other things.

As noted before, you need to consider the cost. Unless the course is advertised as free of charge, it's likely you'll be spending some bucks

---

*Accreditation is the process by which an external body evaluates the services, courses, and operations of an educational institution to determine whether or not they meet a set of standards. If standards are met, accreditation is granted to the institution.

on it—and for any books or materials needed as well. If a course is offered by a local college, it's certainly worth checking to see if financial aid is available. You should also determine if you'll need to pay for everything up front or if it's possible to pay in installments on a monthly or quarterly basis.

Finally, think about the time your student will have to devote to successfully complete the course. If you go through the search process and the course is approved by your daughter's high school, will she still have to keep the same course load or will she be able to substitute the outside course for one on her normal schedule? If she must keep the same course load during the school week, how much time will she have to devote to the supplemental course after homework and her other activities? You will have to weigh all of the various factors when making this important decision. You and your child may decide that it's better for her to take a supplemental course or two over the summer rather than during an active school year.

Finally, as noted before, take a look at the list of recommended resources in the back of the book. There you will find links to sites offering study aids, tutoring assistance, and more.

Discussing College Majors

I know what you are thinking. Why in the world are we discussing college majors in the ninth grade? You're right—it is early. I don't expect your student to find a major or decide on a career in ninth grade, but I do think it's a good idea for them to start thinking about it.

Choosing a major can be hard work. There are many factors involved, such as passions, abilities, aptitude, future earning potential, employment outlook, and more. But let's start with considering what your child likes or loves to do: their passion.

Do You Know What Your Child's Passion Is?

It's been said that when you're doing something you love, it doesn't feel like work. I'm sure there's some truth to that. However, when you're a high school student or incoming college freshman, do you really know what your passion is? I know adults who are still trying to find their passion. Your child may not call it passion. I wouldn't call it passion either.

You know your teen. The focus should be on what lights him or her up inside. Passion is supposed to be that thing a person can do over and over and never get tired. That isn't something you *find*, it's something you *know*. Your child already knows what that is, and so do you. Adults are looking for their passion because somewhere on the path they lost their way. Your child is just beginning. The best way we can assist our children is to remember who they are and how they got there. Passion and purpose is in that place. In the end, we just hope it's something at which they can make a living. Here are some ways you can help your child explore who he or she is, and, hopefully, that can lead to a potential college major.

Relevant Questions

Ask your child to think about the things he or she likes to do. Ask your child for specifics. Here are some examples of conversation starters:

- Give a speech or write a speech?
- Actor or director?
- Listen to music or play music?
- Plan everything out or dive right in?
- Keep it to yourself or share it with others?
- Reinvent the wheel or improve upon something that already exists?
- Leader or team member?
- Solitude or do you prefer being in a room full of people?

- Are you comfortable in social situations?

- Talk it out or write it out?

The goal of this exercise is to begin to zero in on your child's passion by matching activities or majors to their individual personality, rather than making them choose from a limited menu of what happens to be popular. We tend to stick to the same majors and same ideas rather than matching the student's personality and interest to their potential field. Even if this conversation doesn't lead to an epiphany, it can help you narrow down some potential activities to explore with your child that can eventually lead your child down the path to a major.

- What do local recreation centers or parks have to offer? They might have interesting nonacademic courses, such as a drama production course that could teach your child how to do everything in a theater production from writing the play to building the set.

- Is there a Habitat for Humanity project or a soup kitchen in your area? See if your child can volunteer—you can even do this with your child. This may appeal to a service-oriented child, and the experience expands your child's résumé.

- Think about what your child likes. A friend of mine has a daughter who loves anything and everything that has to do with flowers. The perfect summer job for her was at the flower store. The hours were limited, but she learned everything about something she already loved. At the end, her daughter even planted flowers around the yard. Perhaps one day she will be an awesome botanist.

Once you have some of the answers written out, figure out if the answers match with any of the courses your child is currently taking. If your child is logic-based, and abstract thought processes make no sense to him or her, it may make sense that math is a favorite subject. These responses may also help you with creating a current course schedule.

There are certainly plenty of books out on the market to help with this. One book you might want to check out is Peterson's *Making*

Your Major Decision, which uses personality insights to help a student choose his or her major. Written with the folks at CPP, the makers of the Myers-Briggs Type Indicator® (MBTI®), the guide offers information about personality characteristics and work and learning styles that are part of one's academic and career choices. There's also access to an online personality assessment (YourMajorDecision. com) as well as descriptions of more than 800 college majors, including course requirements, related majors, and related careers to help students make their "major decision." Again, we'll discuss choosing a major a bit more in depth later in the book.

Students often choose a major or career based on electives they took in high school. So be mindful of your child's passions, interests, and goals when creating his or her course schedule.

Course Planning Template and Tips

Once you and your student have explored some possible majors and researched what is required academically to pursue those majors, it's time to work on their college-prep curriculum.

To create a college-prep curriculum, gather the following:

- Any standardized test results you have available
- Your student's report cards for the past two years
- Any important notes from teachers regarding your child's progress or academic standing for the past two years
- The proposed course schedule for the current academic year (if you can get all four years, even better)
- A list of all academic support options available at the school
- A list of all electives available at the school and course descriptions, if available
- Notes on your personal observations of your student's strengths and weaknesses
- Input from your child on his or her academic standing and areas that need improvement

As you review these documents, you might see some trends. For example, it is unlikely that your student's challenges in math began in his or her current class. Take a look at their track record and determine if there are any areas that need help.

Now it's time to map out courses.

Step 1: Break down your student's schedule by semester or quarter, depending on how the school's academic schedule is structured.

Step 2: Print out a blank calendar and write in each core class your student will take for the year.

Step 3: Select electives based on areas in which your student needs help. For example, if your son is not a strong writer, one elective course you may want him to consider is creative writing. Another option is a logical reasoning/critical thinking–based course to help him with idea development.

Step 4: Scout out any study hall periods or other downtime available in the schedule. If academic support is available at your school, schedule it during a study hall. See if a school-based tutor or an outside tutor can work with your student during that time. At the end of each grading period, review your student's progress, and determine whether any adjustments need to be made. Keep any new test results, teacher comments, and grade reports in the above-mentioned file.

The following is a sample schedule for a student in Grade 9 (Semester 1):

Period	Class
1	College-Prep English I
2	Algebra I
3	Science
Lunch	
4	P.E./Health
5	Spanish
6	Elective

Grade 10 (Semester 1):

Period	Class
1	College-Prep English II
2	Advanced Math
3	College-Prep World History
Lunch	
4	College-Prep Biology
5	Spanish II
6	P.E.

Grade 11 (Semester 1):

Period	Class
1	College-Prep English III
2	AP Math
3	College-Prep U.S. History
Lunch	
4	Chemistry
5	Spanish III
6	Elective

It's Winter . . . Better Plan for Summer!

Your child's college application will one day be competing against those of other students. Sometimes, as a parent, you don't have as much control as you would like over the courses offered at your child's school. This is when the summer can become a valuable opportunity in your child's path to college. You can help your student make the most of his or her summer following ninth grade by strengthening their talents and skills or making up for some academic weaknesses you spotted during the school year. It can be particularly useful if you want your son or daughter to get ahead of the curriculum and take some core classes so that he or she has the flexibility during the academic year to skip ahead on the math track or take some advanced-level courses. For a more in-depth discussion on great options for your student during the summers after ninth grade, check out **Chapter 7—Summer: An Important Part of Your Student's College Plan.**

Now that you've gotten to know your student's guidance counselor, worked through course planning, and hopefully checked out summer programs, it's time for some heavy lifting—saving for college.

Building a Résumé

Résumés aren't just for job applicants! Even in high school, your child needs one, and ninth grade is a great time to start keeping a working list of his or her accomplishments. It can be difficult for anyone to recall each of their accomplishments at a moment's notice. However, recalling their accomplishments is exactly what your child will have to do over and over again as he or she fills out applications for college or extracurricular programs, prepares for admission interviews, applies for scholarships, and applies for that first job. Having an easy-to-reference résumé can ensure your son or daughter doesn't forget the important stuff!

You can help your child draft a traditional résumé or you can use an online platform to do so, however, I wouldn't recommend paying for it. Even though it may seem premature, your student can begin working on this as early as ninth grade. Some students start looking for outside employment as young as age 15 or 16, so it's important for them to see how everything they've done makes them interesting and viable candidates. Creating a résumé helps them gather all those pieces of information that they'll need for college, scholarship, and even employment applications. Once they start listing the things they've done and achieved, they will probably be surprised! It's easy to create a document on the computer and then revise it or update it with new accomplishments.

As adults, we think of a résumé as an employment history, but your student's resume might look a little different. So what should be in a student's résumé? Here are some ideas:

- Educational history: the school your child attends, his or her grade level, additional academic programs, and any college plans
- Extracurricular activities and the duration he or she participated in those activities, both school- and community-based
- Honors and achievements: academic honors, awards for extracurricular activities, programs that your student was accepted into, scholarships, and so on
- Community service: brief descriptions of ongoing volunteer involvement
- Work history: any part-time employment—even if it's just babysitting, mowing lawns, or dog walking—demonstrates responsibility and work ethic

Generally, a high school student's résumé should only include things they have completed during those years. Winning the second-grade spelling bee was terrific, but that achievement is long past its expiration date.

Saving for College

Confession: I had one undergraduate loan for $10,000. Here's my story: My mother wanted me to go to Oakwood University in Huntsville, Alabama. I didn't want to go. She already had me graduating in a senior class of 18 students from an extremely small Christian academy. I wasn't about to go to its university counterpart for my undergraduate studies. No way.

Then she said the magic words, "If you go to Oakwood, I'll pay your tuition." Um, what? Clearly, I went to Oakwood.

When I committed to Oakwood, my mother and I made a deal. I would study incredibly hard and would bring my ACT score up to where it needed to be for me to be eligible for a scholarship. Mom said she would cover the rest.

I did not receive a full scholarship—not by any stretch of the imagination. However, I was able to earn enough scholarship money to cover about half of my tuition. My mother's savings (an amount that is a secret to this day) covered the rest. The only reason I needed to take out the $10,000 loan was because I wanted to live off campus during my junior and senior years, and that wasn't a part of the original bargain.

You can plan to save a lot of money. In fact, you can save every spare penny you have. Yet, few parents these days are able to save enough money to cover the entire cost of a four-year college tuition plus room and board costs. According to the nonprofit College Savings Plans Network, the average 529 College Savings Plan account reached only $19,584 in 2013. For most colleges and universities, that amount doesn't even cover one academic year.

The good news is that you don't need to pay your child's full tuition. The reality is that your planning and savings can put a significant dent in your child's potential reliance on student loans or the size of those loans.

It can be done. I am a testament to that fact, as are thousands of others. For more information on saving for college, check out **Chapter 6—Financial Fundamentals: Planning and Paying for College.**

Steps in the Right Direction

At this point, you should have a lot more information to help you navigate your child's ninth-grade year and the years ahead. You've spoken to your child's guidance counselor and created a plan to make sure your student is on the right path to college. You are becoming aware of the many resources available to you inside and outside of your child's high school, as well as how to evaluate whether they will be useful for your child. You have learned about some college savings programs and hopefully started one of your own. You've talked with your child about college majors and explored his or her passions. Congratulations! You've gotten a great start on sending your child off to college.

NINTH-GRADE CHECKLIST

Questions to Answer before Ninth Grade

☐ Have you called your child's high school to determine if his or her guidance counselor has been assigned?

☐ If no counselor has been assigned yet, do you know when the school will assign the counselor?

☐ Have you asked when the first semester schedule will be finalized?

☐ If your school has assigned a counselor, have you called to schedule an appointment prior to the start of school, if possible?

☐ If your school's guidance counselor isn't available prior to the start of school, have you made an appointment within the first two weeks of school?

Questions to Ask Your Student's Guidance Counselor

☐ What percentage of students at your school graduates from high school?

☐ At your school, what percentage of students attends college upon graduation?

☐ What are the average scores on the ACT, SAT, and PSAT/NMSQT exams?

☐ On average, are there any subjects that present test problems for students at the school?

☐ Does the school offer the ACT Plan and Explore in addition to the PSAT/NMSQT to students in grades 9 and 10?

☐ Can the counselor provide you with a copy of your child's proposed ninth-grade course schedule?

☐ Does the school offer academic support programs for struggling students and in what subjects?

☐ Does the school offer general, vocational or tech-prep, and college-prep diplomas?

☐ Can the counselor provide you with a copy of your school's graduation requirements for a college-prep diploma?

☐ Can the counselor provide you with a copy of a sample college-prep academic course schedule?

☐ Does the school offer Advanced Placement (AP) or International Baccalaureate (I.B.) courses?

☐ What courses does the counselor recommend for a college-bound student?

☐ What are the prerequisite courses for the more challenging courses on the college-prep schedule, and is there a minimum GPA requirement for those courses?

☐ Does the counselor recommend any local summer programming for a college-bound student?

Questions to Answer during the Ninth-Grade Year

☐ Does your student's class schedule put him or her on track to meet the basic graduation requirements for the state?

☐ If you plan on enrolling your child in advanced courses, is he or she on track to take the prerequisites for each of those advanced courses?

☐ Does your child have a mix of academic and practical electives in his or her schedule?

☐ Have you determined what the requirements are for your child to be enrolled in A.P or I.B. courses?

☐ Have you discussed dual enrollment opportunities with your child's guidance counselor?

☐ Have you researched local options for college-prep or supplemental courses for your child?

☐ Have you had the 'major' conversation with your child?

☐ Have you and your child researched volunteer and/or academic opportunities for the upcoming summer?

☐ Have you researched and chosen a college savings plan for your family?

CHAPTER 2

Tenth Grade: Preparing Now Pays Off Later

Tenth grade can be an oddball year. Students who started high school in ninth grade have adapted to their surroundings and feel a bit more confident now that they're not the lowest on the food chain anymore. But for other students, it's their first year in a high school, so they're adjusting to a new building, new schedules, and new extracurricular opportunities. And besides, graduation is still two years away, so there's plenty of time to plan for college, right?

Wrong! Your student's junior and senior years will be very busy with college-preparation activities. It's important to avoid a sophomore slump in planning for the future. There's a lot of groundwork that can be done during tenth grade to make progress on his or her journey.

Here are some important things to focus on during tenth grade:

- Maintaining grades
- Continuing to discuss and explore potential college majors
- Planning a productive summer
- Reviewing test preparation

Working On a Major—Yes, a Major!

"When I grow up, I want to be… I have no idea." Sound familiar? This section will help you get closer to replacing your student's "I have no idea!" with something solid and positive.

In the spirit of full disclosure, I am not a big fan of tests or assessments to determine a career choice. I believe that most people know who they are and what they are supposed to be doing in life, but we have so much clutter in our heads that we often can't even hear our own voices. I think your child knows, deep down, somewhere. Maybe it's not a trendy new profession, or what you want to hear, or the job that will make enough money to pay back student loans, but he or she knows. Okay, now I'll step down off my soapbox.

Truthfully, an assessment or test is just a starting point. It will help to spark a discussion with your child and prod him or her toward self-discovery. In addition, once you discuss potential career options with your child, you can also begin exploring majors and options with your student's guidance counselor. So let's get into it.

Career Aptitude Tests

Perhaps I wasn't being fair in stating that I don't like assessments. I have taken some work-related assessments that were pretty accurate. For example, the Myers-Briggs Type Indicator was dead-on for me. If you can find a well-researched, widely used assessment, it may give you some insight into your child's aspirations.

There are dozens of assessments available online; some of them are even free. Here are a few assessments that can give you an idea of what majors might be a good fit for your student.

Jung Typology Test (www.humanmetrics.com/cgi-win/JungType. htm): This is similar to the Myers-Briggs Type indicator. It helps to define your student's personality type formula, and it offers a career indicator test, which suggests possible career choices based on that personality type.

Keirsey Temperament Sorter (www.keirsey.com/sorter/register. aspx): This can be a good indicator of your student's likes and dislikes, which can then lead you to explore careers that fit his or her personality type.

The MAPP™ Career Assessment Test (www.assessment.com): This website indicates that more than 7 million people have taken the 15-minute MAPP career test—that's a lot of people. You can get a sample report and five possible career matches for free, but there is a cost for additional information. However, it may be worth it given the reports and analysis the test report provides.

Personality Test for High School Students (www.high-school. devry.edu/personality-profile/questions.htm): This website offers career guides specific to high school students. It offers growth statistics for particular fields of study as well as an online personality profile with recommendations for various personality types.

Your state's department of labor or workforce development website may offer online tests to determine interests and possible career paths, and these tests are often free for state residents. Your student's guidance counselor may be able to refer you to these or other sites more specific to your town, city, state, or part of the country.

Once you have identified some possible career areas, you and your student can use the power of the Internet to learn more, such as the demand for such jobs, education level and majors required for those careers, earning potential, and so on. There is an abundance of this kind of information; some of it can be found on individual colleges' websites as they detail what professional opportunities await potential students if they pursue a particular major. Here are two other good starting points:

- **U.S. Bureau of Labor Statistics** (http://www.bls.gov/ooh/): The Occupational Outlook Handbook lets you browse and check out information on hundreds of occupations.

- **Education Planner** (educationplanner.org): This website offers interactive exercises with to-the-point instructions to help your child prepare for important decisions like choosing a major. This site is a public service of the Pennsylvania Higher Education Assistance Agency, FedLoan Servicing, and American Education Services.

Just keep in mind that these sites are simply tools to get you started, spark discussion, and provide direction. The hard work in choosing a major isn't going to be on the assessment/testing end, but rather on the research end. There are so many careers from which to choose. Students who fail to do the research may never find one that suits them. And careers are changing all the time—while new ones appear, too. For instance, an interesting career that has popped up in the last five years is a trend spotter.

A trend spotter is someone who specializes in identifying emerging trends in various industries. Many trend spotters work in fashion, but the career has recently appeared in computing, technology, and other fields. Spotters have to know and understand how trends emerge and have a keen understanding of people. But what do trend spotters major in? Are there entry-level trend spotter positions? Who made this up and how did they start? Were you even aware that this career existed? Imagine how many other amazing and fun careers are out there.

Keep Your Guidance Counselor in the Loop

Reaching out to students to talk about their futures can be difficult. My high school counselor, Ms. Harris, chased most of us down the hallway to get a meeting with us. I hid behind my locker as she screamed my name down the small corridor. She seemed like the big bad wolf. Don't pity her though. My graduating class consisted of about 18 students, so Ms. Harris didn't have too many of us to keep up with. However, your student may attend a school where the guidance counselor is assigned to hundreds of students, and that counselor certainly won't have the time to chase a student down the hall. In addition, remember that each school's policies and procedures regarding student-counselor contact vary; some students have to initiate all meetings and contact, while other schools may have mandatory meetings between students and their counselors a few times a year.

That's why I continue to suggest that *you* reach out to the counselor to make things easier and to forge a solid partnership. The guidance counselor is going to be the entry point and college admissions expert at your school. Information about special opportunities, programs, scholarships, and area colleges is all going to come via the guidance counselor. If you and your student have established a relationship with the counselor, it's more likely that counselor may think of your student as a candidate for those opportunities.

Set up an appointment with your child and the counselor. But ideally, you should not be at this meeting because I want your child to freely discuss his or her ideas and aspirations. I was completely honest with my parents about what I wanted to do and what school I wanted to go to. However, not every student is comfortable being so open with their parents because they often fear the perceived response. If students have the opportunity to share without their parents there, they may reveal some things to their counselors about their aspirations that can impact planning for college and beyond.

Before the appointment, you and your child should write down some questions to ask. For example: If I like to draw, what kind of careers should I look into? What colleges in the region offer the particular major I'm considering? Students should request suggested resources that they can follow up on, whether they're books, websites, or after-school or summer programs specific to those interests. Have your son or daughter brainstorm before the meeting and go in armed with questions, so that he or she can leave with a good amount of information and action items.

Even after going through all these steps, keep in mind that the conclusion to your student's "When I go to college I want to study…" sentence may still be "I don't know!" While it may be easier to have a specific major in mind when applying to colleges, many applicants—statistics indicate as many as 50 percent—check the "undecided" box on the list of majors. Colleges know that students today are often conflicted about a choice of majors. For example, Drexel University tailors programs specifically for what the school calls "still-deciding students" while Lawrence University chooses the term "multi-interested" instead of "undecided" on its application. To help its "undecided" students, Penn State University Park offers a special-interest residence hall for freshmen called Discover House, which provides special programs and extra advising to help students investigate and choose their academic major and career.

Finally, remember that a major chosen in tenth grade is subject to change. Binge-watching *CSI* episodes may convince your daughter that forensic science is what she wants to study, but a year from now, a favorite teacher's class may have her saying she wants to pursue a history degree. Majoring in math may sound great to your son when he's in tenth grade, but struggling mightily with senior-year calculus could cause him to change his mind. And the reality is that 50 to 70 percent of students change their major at least once during college. So just as your student's favorite musical group and clothing styles can change from year to year, so can his or her potential major. But it's still important that your child thinks about, talks about, and researches some possibilities.

Maintaining a High GPA

Let's be realistic. Maintaining a high GPA in high school is no easy task. It requires organization, hard work, and effective time management on your student's part. You are probably busy—most parents are, particularly if you have more than one child. Factor in your job, your children's extracurricular activities, family commitments, and managing a household—and your time is spent! It will be difficult to stay on top of all of your student's tests and homework. However, there is hope. Working with your child on some of the following strategies can put him or her on track to maintaining a solid GPA and developing the skills needed to succeed in college.

Keep the Momentum Going toward a Strong Finish

Sanya Richard-Ross has been running track since she was 7 years old. In 2004, at age 19, she became a professional track athlete while just a sophomore in college. During that year, Richard-Ross was a member of the U.S. Olympic team that won the gold medal in the 4x400-meter relay race. By the time she got to the 2008 Olympic Games in Beijing, Richard-Ross qualified faster than any other competitor in the world for the finals and was the favorite to win the gold on her own in the 400m race.

Richard-Ross was arguably the best runner on the field that day. She should have gone home with a gold medal. Instead, she went home with the bronze. What happened? She came out of the blocks too quickly, and by the time she got to the finishing straight, she lacked the power she needed to accelerate across the finish line and take home the gold.

In 2012, she wouldn't make the same mistake. Richard-Ross came steady out of the starting blocks and was even passed by other runners. Then she hit the finishing stretch. She accelerated past each and every runner on the track, including the defending champion who had won that same race in 2008, to take home the gold once and for all in 49.55 seconds. For Richard-Ross, having a great start and maintaining a strong momentum throughout the race—all the way to the finish line—made all the difference, the difference between a gold and bronze medal.

Students may not win Olympic gold, silver, or bronze medals, but how they start their year and maintain their momentum from September through June (or August through May) is crucial toward attaining the strong GPA and college-prep skills they need.

At the beginning of the fall semester, many students are still shaking off the back-to-school blues. They do their homework, but studying isn't really their main focus. Their real attempts at studying often only kick in when it's time to prepare for midterm exams. But many students suddenly realize that they haven't paid enough attention in class or worked hard enough on assignments. So they do what they can to make up for it toward the end of the semester. Then, after the midterm grades come in and shock the system, cramming for finals begins. It's hardly the way to "run that gold-medal race" through the school year, and, despite the best late attempts, it often equals a lousy finish.

Students who start the semester strong build a foundation for the entire semester through consistency—doing each homework assignment and earning extra credit whenever it's available. That important head start allows them to manage midterms and finals more easily. I hate to state the obvious, but the higher the grade your student has in a class, the more flexible a teacher may be should any problems arise during midterms or final exams. For example, let's say your daughter, who has an A in algebra, isn't feeling great on the day of her algebra midterm. Her math teacher will already know the high quality of her schoolwork and may be able to accommodate her illness that day and perhaps even give an extra point or two if necessary.

If your child needs monitoring or a little guidance to ensure that his or her schoolwork is completed, I would encourage you to be diligent about this during the beginning of each semester. If your student has a weak start to the semester, it will take a lot more effort and energy to recover during the middle and end of it. As noted before, a strong start isn't going to guarantee that your student will "win the gold," but with continued strong strides—and the following tips—hopefully, it will help him or her have an outstanding school year.

Friends Who Study Together Graduate Together

There are dozens of academic studies that discuss the value of having your child participate in a study group. If you think study groups are great, you can surely find a study or statistic that supports that point of view, and vice versa. I would agree that there can be enormous value in studying in a group. However, if your child is as talkative and easily distracted as I am, he or she may need to study alone. Keeping in mind how your child operates and interacts with people, school, friends, and teachers is a good way to gauge whether or not group study will work.

If your student has a group of focused friends who are potential study partners, it may be a good idea to have them occasionally study together. There are several potential benefits to having your child work in a study group:

- **Creating Ideas:** When students work as a team and their creative juices start flowing, they often come up with great new thoughts and ideas.

- **Filling in the Gaps:** Surely, someone in the group may look at the lesson from a different perspective, which can help your student look at the lesson in a new way. Other group members may have picked up on something that your child missed or be able to explain something that your child found confusing.

- **Building Healthy Competition:** One of my students had a great study-buddy. Aside from studying together for quizzes and tests, they would compete with each other to see who could get the higher grade on the test or class assignment. When one did well, the other would congratulate him. When one didn't understand something, the other would help explain it. Both students graduated at the top of their high school class, within a few tenths of a point separating their GPAs.

- **Targeting Specific Assignments:** When there's little time to study together for an exam or to complete a group assignment, there's also little time for chit-chat, texting, or checking Facebook—common distractions. In these situations, students in a study group learn they need to keep their eye on the prize.

As just noted, a potential and common pitfall to progress in a study group is the temptation to socialize. Speaking from experience, I was a social child, who grew into a social adult. I've never been able to work in study group, even when I was in law school. Too often, I was the one who would start discussing anything and everything—except for the important topic at hand. So, I learned that study groups were not for me, and my previous study mates wholeheartedly agreed.

If you aren't sure whether or not group study will be beneficial for your student, you could do a trial run when your child has a minor test or small group project. Host a study or group-assignment session at your home. While you won't want to eavesdrop too conspicuously, you should check in every now and then to determine that the conversation is staying on track. If you see that the group is staying focused and things are getting accomplished, you'll know that your student should be fine studying for a bigger exam with this group of students. However, if you pop in the room and discover they're talking about the upcoming school dance, and most of the study group members are checking out the latest cool video on their phones, you'll know that study groups may not be the best idea for your student. As with all things, your guidance and direction does matter.

Go to Class and Go Above and Beyond

I cannot stress enough the importance of going to class. So much happens in class: lectures, discussion, group work, questions from other students, interaction with the instructor, and, of course, that's where assignments and due dates are given. There are many factors that impact when, how, and why a student learns, but ideally, a huge part of that learning should happen inside of the classroom. However, it won't happen passively, and just being present in the classroom doesn't guarantee learning. It takes effort to learn.

A large factor in classroom learning is participation. When students listen attentively, respond to questions, and actively take part in classroom discussion, they demonstrate to the instructor that they are attempting, at least, to understand the material and are actively engaged in learning. High-quality classroom interactions can often awaken a child's intellectual curiosity. The objective of education is always to promote understanding rather than rote memorization. However, with the current emphasis on standardized testing in some school districts and states, requiring instructors to teach 'to the test' rather than for understanding, memorization of certain facts, figures, and formulas is often the result. This is precisely why it is essential to not depend on classroom learning. What happens outside of the classroom—at home, in supplemental programs, in extracurricular activities, and in everyday life—can be just as important.

One of my students, Nathan, had an incredible memory. Anything I explained to him could be repeated back to me verbatim. He had a 3.5 GPA, so no one ever questioned whether or not he really understood what he could repeat. But when he didn't perform well on the ACT, his parents were in shock, and they hired me to tutor him.

After a few sessions, a pattern emerged. Nathan could retain information but he wasn't able to apply what he 'learned' when the context was different. For example, when he memorized a formula, it had to appear in the same way that he had learned it in order for him to get the question correct. So had he truly learned anything if he couldn't apply the formula in a different context? In an effort to help figure out what Nathan had learned and what he hadn't, I worked with him in two areas: comprehension and application.

To help him with comprehension, I had Nathan translate what he memorized into his own words. I thought that if he could convert the memorized material into sentences he would use, he stood a better chance of truly understanding the concept. He hated it in the beginning because it took a lot of effort for him to articulate his thoughts without simply mimicking what he had previously heard. He would have to try again and again.

When he was stumped, I would ask him questions about the concept or do a few more problems to jog his memory and provide a foundation to discuss why and how the concept should be applied. Once we worked through the questions, he started to understand what it meant to translate the material into his own words and explain what he was doing.

Then, to help with application, Nathan practiced. He would complete and review dozens of problems to see if he could apply what he learned and figure out what he was doing wrong and why. Then he would try a different problem, not repeating the same mistake. Once he got the hang of translating and reworking problems and concepts, he began using those techniques successfully in his classwork, and his ACT scores increased dramatically.

But just as every child is different, the process needed to truly learn what they hear in the classroom will also vary from child to child. If your son is struggling, it may take considerable effort on your part to determine why and then find the help he needs beyond the classroom. Much of it also depends on how motivated your student is—your child has to want it, too.

For many students, following this basic **four-step model** is a good starting point to help them remember and solidify what they learn at school.

1) Listen and participate in class.

2) Come home and do the homework assignment.

3) Turn in the homework, and receive correction from the instructor.

4) Review mistakes, correct them, and practice again.

These four steps are just a starting point. Once students are comfortable with the process, what they do beyond these basic steps will help them move toward a deeper understanding and permanent integration of the material.

Note-Taking

Notes are far more than just words on paper; they can be the tool that streamlines studying and helps ensure success in just about every class. But unfortunately, many students have never learned when, why, or how to take effective notes.

So when should your student take notes? More than he or she might think! Top students take notes while reading the text assignments and again while the teacher is lecturing in class. If there's a little time before they need to rush to the next class, great students use those few minutes to write a two- or three-sentence summary of the lesson's key points so that information isn't lost as soon as they leave the classroom. Sometimes students don't take the time to read everything assigned by the teacher or don't take time after class to digest the information they received during the lecture. So, good note-taking can be a lifesaver—in high school and even more so in college.

Here's why note-taking is important. First, if a student is a good note-taker, it means that most of the time he or she is actually paying attention in class. Taking good notes requires students to actively listen, process the information, and then write it down. Secondly, students' notes provide the foundation when they need to study for tests. They don't have to guess what material was covered by the teacher—it's all in their notes.

Good note-taking is another study skill that your student may have to work to develop; it doesn't just happen. Here are some tips you can share with your student. Make sure your child understands them, and help him or her to practice.

Note-Taking Tips to Share with Your Student

- Make sure your student reads the assigned material before class and takes notes while doing so. Hopefully there is a syllabus or some sort of schedule to direct him or her. Completing the reading before class will guide your student's note-taking as well as his or her understanding of the classroom discussion.

- Students can't take notes if they don't have the tools, so they have to bring what is needed to class. It drove me nuts when students came to my prep class without a pencil, pen, or notebook paper. What kind of student shows up unprepared? The kind who isn't prepared to learn. That should not be your student.

- Taking notes does *not* mean writing everything down. Students aren't supposed to be court reporters. Instead, they should actively listen. Teachers will usually repeat the important material or emphasize the high points. Things that a teacher repeats or spends a significant amount of time on are probably worth writing down. With practice, your student will develop a discerning ear.

- Even when noting key points, your student doesn't need to write it down verbatim. Help train your student to use short sentences or paraphrase, without changing the meaning.

- Double space the notes. While we usually think of double spacing on typed material, it makes sense to do it when taking handwritten notes, too. That extra space provides room to expand on the material after class, make corrections, or fill in the gaps when something is missing. It's hard to read tiny notes that are squeezed into the margins afterwards.

- If possible, review the notes immediately after class, and fill in anything that may not have been captured during class time (yes, that's where the double spacing comes in handy). It's best to fill in the gaps while the lecture is fresh in your student's mind.

- Review the notes regularly—not just when it's time to cram for a test. They can clarify homework and make it easy to review for exams.

Help Your Student's Interests and Talents Shine Through

As your child matriculates through high school and beyond, you will hear frequent talk about how a student should be well-rounded. By virtue of its overuse, it almost seems like "well-rounded" is a buzzword, with no functional or practical meaning. Are schools asking you to raise Mother Teresa, Albert Einstein, and Will Smith, all in one child? No. At a minimum, college applicants are academically viable students. GPAs don't need to be perfect, but for the sake of argument, let's assume students will be rejected if they don't meet some minimum viability. Let's add in test scores. If we have a student who has a competitive GPA and solid test scores, then what's left? A lot!

When people say colleges want well-rounded students, I think they have it all wrong. Colleges want a well-rounded freshman class, meaning students of diverse backgrounds and with varying interests, because that's what the real world looks like, right? So while this book focuses on encouraging you to help your child maintain a solid GPA and score high on standardized tests, I also encourage you to let your child stand out by participating in activities and programs he or she is passionate about.

What if you saw a résumé from a job applicant who changed jobs every year? Then you noticed that each job was in a different field. One year it was computer science, and the next year it was public relations. What would you think of the applicant? Is this person "well-rounded" or just unfocused? Would you hire such an applicant? Perhaps not.

Justin Ball, Associate Vice President for Enrollment Management at Bradley University, says that when his team is reviewing applications, they are trying to determine whether students are a good fit for the community and culture of the university. He adds that extracurricular activities aren't limited to those that are school-based.

He notes, "Admissions offices want to hear about a student's accomplishments and abilities. This can range from leading a club or organization—like Key Club, National Honor Society, or the Fellowship of Christian Athletes—to outstanding awards such as Eagle Scout, Most Improved Player, or State Honor Band—to personal victories such as overcoming a disability, managing caring for a parent or sibling while being successful in school, or dedicating time to a particular charity or cause."

Sarah E. Gibbs, Director of Admissions at Grove City College in Pennsylvania, says that she looks for the type of involvement each student has had in leadership, volunteer work, music, and/or athletics in order to get a glimpse of the whole student. Ms. Gibbs adds that no school wants to set a student up for failure by admitting someone who wouldn't fit in well on its campus. To best determine whether a student will "fit," admission deans and directors need to have an authentic look at who the young man or woman is—beyond the test scores and GPA.

The possibilities in this arena are endless. Let's look at some options that may work for your student.

Extracurricular Activities

Extracurricular is much broader than parents traditionally think, and it truly includes anything your child participates in that isn't required by curriculum. Like most of us, your child will be more motivated to participate in an activity that he or she likes, not one that is forced. So, since the activity options aren't limited to academic, sports, or leadership activities, why not allow your student to figure out what he or she likes?

SO MUCH TO CHOOSE FROM AND SO MUCH TO GAIN. There are so many activities your child can choose from, inside and outside of school. Many of them probably didn't exist when you were in school—anime clubs, soccer teams, Model UN, computer clubs—all reflective of changing times and the interests of today's students. Ask your school's guidance counselor for a list of clubs and activities at school or have your student reach out to a representative from the student government for a list. Look for opportunities in your community, too, through the local newspaper, library, community center, or your place of worship.

Keep in mind that extracurricular activities can be yet another way to help a student identify their passion. As mentioned before, many students choose a major in college based on a course or an activity from high school.

There seemed to be something magical about the Smith family; all eight of them, living and thriving under one roof. I met them because I was hired to tutor Jerrod, the youngest son. Jerrod was in the twelfth grade and wanted to increase his ACT score so he could get a scholarship to the Naval Academy (a goal that he accomplished, by the way). In addition to ACT tutoring, Jerrod was a track star, participated in R.O.T.C., was active in his church, worked at the family business, and maintained a 3.5 GPA. How in the world did he do all that? Apparently, it ran in the family. His older siblings were either in college or had graduated from college, and his younger sister was just as busy in high school, maintaining a B average while also on the track team.

I sat down with Mrs. and Mr. Smith to ask how they kept that many children in line. Mrs. Smith's response was simple—she said she didn't have to. The Smiths had a delivery company and put each of the children to work at the family business in some way at a very young age. In addition, each of the eight children started competing in track in elementary school. Mr. Smith added that they didn't have to monitor their kids' homework because it was the family's expectation that schoolwork was to be done, no questions asked.

The older children also set the example for the younger ones to follow, and no one wanted to be the one Smith child with bad grades. Furthermore, the discipline they learned at a young age from working and being a part of an organized sport helped each of them learn time management and responsibility. Mr. and Mrs. Smith also credited participation in extracurricular activities for their children's discipline and success.

Being part of a team—whether it's the football team or the chess team—can teach your student commitment and leadership skills as well as how to work collaboratively. In addition, juggling both class schedules and activity schedules can help your child develop time-management and prioritization skills.

CHOOSE WISELY. With so many potential activities to take part in, your student has to make some decisions. Your child can't do it all, and you should help him or her work through those choices.

What is the time commitment for each activity: daily, weekly, throughout the school year, or just during a season? Will it require a few hours each day after school and competitions on the weekends, or is it just one evening a week? Will practice last well beyond dinnertime and cut into your child's homework time? How will your student balance the activity with his or her course load?

When your student does commit to an activity, encourage your child to stick with it for more than one year. This gives him or her the opportunity to rise into a leadership position and reflects consistency and commitment when it's time to put that activity on a college application. Admissions officers would rather see a student thoroughly commit to one or two activities for all four years of high school than an array of one-year involvements in various activities.

You can also use extracurricular activities as motivation to ensure that your student stays focused on their school work. If your child's grades are good but suddenly drop once basketball season starts, that's a red flag that some adjustments need to be made. On the other hand, being allowed to do something he or she loves can also be a motivational tool; for example, your daughter might study more diligently if she knows that a subpar grade will jeopardize an opportunity to be in the drama club.

Start Preparing for Testing: Taking the PSAT/NMSQT®

Your student will take the Preliminary SAT/National Merit Scholarship Qualifying Test (PSAT/NMSQT) during the fall of his or her eleventh grade year of high school. Don't fall into the trap of thinking that, because this is a preliminary test, it doesn't matter. Rather than just going in and winging it, your student should be prepared. And that starts with taking a practice test in tenth grade. The PSAT/NMSQT is a program co-sponsored by the College Board and National Merit Scholarship Corporation (NMSC). It's a standardized test that provides firsthand practice for the SAT, the college entrance exam many universities use to assess college readiness.

Like most standardized tests, the PSAT/NMSQT doesn't test knowledge so much as it tests skill. For example, the test doesn't measure if a student knows what 2+2 is. Instead it measures if a student has the skills to correctly answer the question: What is 2+2? In addition, the test doesn't assess whether your child can spell "cat," but whether your child understands the meaning of "cat" in a paragraph. And so on. The exam tests the reading, writing, and math skills your child has developed over the course of his or her academic career.

Key Info About the PSAT/NMSQT

Test dates: Offered on a Wednesday and Saturday, both usually in October

Duration: 2 hours 10 minutes

Sections: Three—math, critical reading, and writing

Maximum score: 80 in each section; 240 overall

Average score: 141

Cost: $14 (but schools may charge an additional administrative fee)

Why is the PSAT/NMSQT Important?

The PSAT/NMSQT is **not** a college entrance exam. However, when taken in eleventh grade, it serves as the qualifying test for National Merit Scholarships. That means that the highest scoring students may win scholarship money. So while students shouldn't stress too much about the PSAT/NMSQT, they shouldn't ignore it, either. Here's why:

- Students' scores on the PSAT/NMSQT are used for awarding many scholarships, including about 8,200 National Merit Scholarships.

- If your student becomes a National Merit finalist (or sometimes even a semifinalist or commended student), he or she may also qualify for other outside scholarships.

- National Merit finalists are often aggressively recruited by colleges. Hundreds of colleges guarantee additional scholarships to National Merit finalists.

While the PSAT/NMSQT is not a college entrance exam it is still a good way to assess your child's grasp of core concepts that will appear on most of the major college readiness tests. Your student will have the opportunity to take the PSAT/NMSQT again in their junior year. But if possible, have your child take it in both tenth and eleventh grade. Taking the PSAT/NMSQT earlier allows you to identify any academic areas that need improvement, so you can focus on those areas during your child's tenth-grade year. Then when your child takes it again in eleventh grade, he or she will be better positioned to do well. And that's when it could mean a large amount of scholarship money.

Taking the test early is also good practice for the tests to come in the years ahead. The experience gives students valuable feedback about what kind of test-takers they are. Were they nervous and jittery or calm and relaxed? Did they freeze up and forget even some basic knowledge because of the perceived stress? These are also areas that can be worked on so that students can be more confident and mentally prepared when they take college entrance tests in the years ahead.

When your student takes the PSAT/NMSQT, he or she can choose to provide name and contact information to colleges looking for potential students. So voilà, colorful brochures and viewbooks will start showing up in your mailbox, along with e-mails as well. While most of the schools might not even be ones that your student would consider, this still provides some early opportunities for you and your student to sit down, look at the materials, and discuss college possibilities.

Staying Strong—No Sophomore Slump!

This chapter was full of information, so I hope you aren't feeling overwhelmed. If you are able to follow some of the advice outlined in this chapter, you will have laid the ground work for your student's success during the finishing stretch of their junior and senior years.

You have now done the following:

- Helped your student to continue thinking about a major and possible careers
- Kept your guidance counselor in the loop so he or she can suggest activities, courses, and opportunities
- Helped your child start their sophomore year strong and maintain solid grades throughout the year by learning specific habits such as note-taking and group study
- Helped find extracurricular activities that will help your child develop academically and socially
- Started planning for the PSAT/NMSQT (if your students hasn't already taken it)

Addressing these items will help your child view tenth grade as an opportunity to make significant progress on his or her college-prep journey.

Please be sure to review **Chapter 7–Summer: An Important Part of Your Student's College Plan** to get some great ideas for the months between your student's sophomore and junior year.

TENTH-GRADE CHECKLIST

Even though graduation may seem far in the future, tenth grade is still an important time to be thinking ahead, planning, and laying the academic groundwork your child will need to go to college. Here's a quick checklist of things you and your child should keep working on this year:

☐ Set up an appointment with your child's guidance counselor to verify that your child is on track with the right courses for the year ahead.

☐ Does your child have a list of five potential choices for a college major?

☐ If not, ask your child to list the top five activities he or she really likes. Based on these favorite activities, create a list of possible majors, and encourage your child to research potential careers associated with each major or activity. The idea here is to start the conversation, not to decide definitively on a major.

☐ If your child is still drawing a blank, consider finding a career-aptitude test for him or her to take.

☐ Encourage your student to set up an appointment with his or her guidance counselor—a meeting *you* won't attend. Help your child prepare for this meeting by writing down questions to ask regarding his or her interests and recommendations the counselor can make about future courses and meaningful activities.

☐ Talk with your student about the importance of maintaining consistent grades throughout the year. Did he or she start the year off strong? Did your student maintain that momentum as the school year moved along?

☐ Discuss the effectiveness of study groups or even a study buddy, and determine if this method would be beneficial for your son or daughter.

☐ Have you shared the note-taking tips included in this chapter with your child? Are there other study habits he or she needs to improve?

☐ Has your child made good choices in terms of extracurricular activities at school or in the community? Has your student committed to sticking with the activity for at least one year?

☐ Do those activities fit with your student's academic schedule—as well as your family's schedule? Is your student able to maintain his or her grades while participating in extracurricular activities?

☐ Did your child take a practice PSAT/NMSQT exam?

☐ Have you and your student determined a meaningful way to spend the summer after tenth grade, such as an enrichment program, a summer job, volunteer work, and so on?

CHAPTER 3

Junior Year: Important Decisions Ahead

COLLEGE BOUND

Congratulations. You're halfway there, but graduation is closer than you think. Junior year is an important time for you to lay the groundwork for college applications. There are some essential activities that should take place this year:

- Your child will take the PSAT/NMSQT® in October, which you hopefully prepared for last school year.

- You should have your student take an early administration of the SAT® and ACT® so that you can see where your child stands and prepare accordingly, if necessary.

- You and your child should visit one or two colleges.

- Your child should begin drafting a college application essay so that there is plenty of time to edit and revise it.

- You and your student should begin making a list of potential recommenders.

- Finally, you and your student should continue determining and researching target colleges and/or universities.

Let's get into it!

Standardized Testing—You Can't Avoid It

No one is born a great test taker. But students can develop good test-taking skills by virtue of their home environment, school, and practice. And as your child prepares to apply to college, taking tests is an unavoidable part of the process.

When I was a child, my mother worked a lot. Often she didn't have time to help with homework. When it came to academics, I was pretty much left on my own. My mom intervened if my grades dipped, but I didn't want to trouble her so I took care of business myself. It wasn't an ideal situation, but she raised an author and a lawyer so I'm guessing she is pretty happy with the outcome.

What she did teach me, among other things, was how to be resourceful. So when I bombed the ACT on the first go-round and was upset with my low score, she asked me, "What are you going to do about it?"

Of course, she already had an answer in mind, but she made me figure it out and get motivated to obtain a better score. She knew that I hated the idea of failing at something, especially tests. I was determined to do better. With that attitude, I was the perfect student.

The perfect student isn't necessarily the one who gets straight A's (honestly, I was a far cry from that!). The perfect student has the desire to learn, is eager to improve, and is willing to put in the work. In my case, I had specific goals to work toward—a higher ACT score and not disappointing my mother—and I was finally willing to do what it took to attain those goals. Moreover, this personal challenge changed how I approached all of my schoolwork, and it made me a better student.

So it's important that your child is motivated to do well on these important college-entrance tests. No test-prep course will help a student who isn't ready to learn.

The first step in test prep is to prepare your child for the hard work ahead. He or she needs to know that this test is important. It took me doing badly on the test to understand that I had to get serious. When your child is ready to prepare, use the tools included in this section to help your child do well.

There seems to be a widespread fear of standardized testing among many students. They don't fear the knowledge that is being tested, but rather the test itself. Most students don't learn the test-taking skills necessary to do well on college entrance exams as part of their traditional schooling. While they may have the knowledge of the material on the tests, they may lack the ability to apply that knowledge in a test-taking situation. So, how do you, as a parent, help your child overcome this fear of testing?

- Encourage your child to develop test-taking skills as early as possible. Chances are they've been exposed to some sort of standardized tests since they started school.

- Plan an early test-taking schedule. Many college entrance tests are offered multiple times throughout the school year. Your student will have multiple opportunities to take those tests. Pick the earliest test date so you can get a baseline assessment of how well your student does on these tests.

- Prepare for the actual test during the spring of your student's junior year. In addition, you can work through testing weaknesses and help your child improve once you know the areas in which he or she is having problems. It's always better to know early, rather than waiting until senior year to fix issues. This section will help you get there.

Getting the Jump on College Entrance Exams

Knowing Your Opponent and Your Student: Tips from the NFL

Former NFL safety, Matt Bowen, once shared some insights into game-week preparation. Bowen noted that on the Monday of game week, both the offense and the defense studied their opponent in the film room. Then, after weightlifting and treatment for injuries, players attended breakout sessions where they studied, reviewed, and highlighted their own mistakes from game film. After approximately 3 hours of looking at the film, the team would head to the field for a correction period. Although the players' day off was on each Tuesday,

Bowen said *that* day was one of the most important of a player's game-week preparation. Why? Because the true pros would be at the training facility, "getting the jump on their opponent" by re-reviewing films or videos, taking notes, identifying the opponents' tendencies and getting a feel for opposing personnel. He adds, "Knowing your team and knowing your opponent were key parts of preparing for the real game."

Students' preparation for their college entrance exams should be similar to what the pro football players do. In a test-prep context, knowing your team and knowing your opponent means your child should know the exam inside and out, be aware of his or her test-taking strengths and weaknesses, and be aware of his or her content strengths and weaknesses. Let's look at those points in a bit more detail:

KNOW THE TEST INSIDE AND OUT: To fully prepare for the ACT or SAT, your child needs to understand what content is being tested and how it is being tested. Each test allows the student to showcase different abilities, yet test-makers also give a predictable range of material to be tested. Even though Bowen and his teammates probably know everything there is to know about football, your child doesn't need to know *everything* there is to know about the SAT or ACT. Still, he or she should know how the exams are structured and the content being tested. We'll get to all that information in the upcoming pages.

BE AWARE OF TEST-TAKING STRENGTHS AND WEAKNESSES: This statement sounds obvious, but it isn't. It takes some effort to figure it out. When I begin tutoring a new student, I always try to find out what the student believes he or she is great at or needs to improve upon.

Kimberly told me that she was horrible at answering math questions—she just hated math. But that didn't ring true because Kimberly was getting B's in her math classes. So I had her take a practice ACT exam to look for the source of her 'math' problem.

I discovered that Kimberly didn't have a math problem—she had an endurance problem. When she came to the practice test she was running late and frazzled. That adrenalin-buzzed state got her through the first 75 questions on the English section of the test, then the McDonald's egg and cheese biscuit she had eaten kicked in by the time she had to tackle the 60 questions on the math section. Kimberly was groggy and unfocused on the math section and ended up with many wrong answers on the types of problem she usually got right in school and on finals.

There's a short break between the first two tests (English and math) and the last two (reading and science). After the break, Kimberly's energy spiked for the reading section but dipped again during science. Contrary to Kimberly's opinion, her problem wasn't math, it was endurance and inconsistency.

So for Kimberly, physical and mental preparation took on more importance. We changed her pre-test breakfast to oatmeal with strawberries. I had her get up and eat breakfast earlier so that by the time she got to the practice test, she had digested her food and she had a steady supply of energy. Finally, she took a practice test once a week for seven weeks to help her adjust to sitting and focusing for an extended period of time. These small tweaks helped Kimberly tremendously. We reinforced her content knowledge in addition to the above strategies, and Kimberly felt the difference.

Watch your child take a practice test, and keep these things in mind:

- Test-taking is as much about endurance as it is about knowledge and skill. Help your child stay alert during the exam by serving a protein- and/or fiber-based breakfast.

- If possible, have your student take a practice test once a week, beginning at least six weeks prior to the exam date.

- Even if you aren't able to determine what his or her test-taking strengths and weaknesses are, you will likely notice other patterns. Most students are consistent. If your child needs help with grammar, he or she will consistently get those questions wrong.

- If you can't detect any problem areas, you may want to have a tutor perform an assessment to see what your child needs to work on.

BE AWARE OF CONTENT-BASED STRENGTHS AND WEAKNESSES: I struggle with the *concept* of test prep because I think it can be misleading. While I believe that test prep can help students learn *how* to take a test well, I'm not convinced that a five- or six-week prep course can help students learn *content* and increase their scores sufficiently to justify the expense to parents. It can happen, but I don't think students or parents should set themselves up to believe that one can re-learn and master concepts that a student may have struggled with for years. Test preparation should be about reviewing content; learning that content should take place in the classroom or with a separate tutor.

With that said, you and your child need to be aware of your child's content-based strengths and weaknesses—not just to prepare for testing but for his or her overall academic success. A practice exam—either self-administered or one of those offered free online or by some test-prep companies—will often reveal which content your student needs to review and strengthen.

Now you and your student need to really dig in and spend some time learning about the opponent your student wants to master—the tests! Here's what you need to know.

The SAT®

If your student will be taking the SAT before March 2016, here are some key points you need to know:

The SAT is considered to be the most widely used college admission test. It was created decades ago by the College Board, a nonprofit education organization, which continues to develop and disburse the exam. The SAT tests students' math, reading, and writing skills—skills that are really important for success in college and life.

Students' scores will be sent to their selected college admission departments. Studies have shown that minorities and students from lower socioeconomic backgrounds are poor performers on the test. So if your child falls within these categories it is good advice to be better prepared.

> ## Key Info About the SAT®
>
> **Test dates:** December, January, March, May, June
>
> **Duration:** 3 hours and 45 minutes
>
> **Sections:** Three—Critical Reading (reading passages and sentence completions); Math (questions on arithmetic operations, algebra, geometry, statistics and probability); and Writing (a short essay and multiple-choice questions on improving grammar and usage and identifying errors)
>
> **Score:** Maximum score is 2400
>
> **Cost:** $51

The SAT is often billed as a test for which you cannot prepare. That's because the SAT is a **REASONING TEST.** It tests how your child thinks, processes information, and works under pressure or time constraints. Your student doesn't need to spend hours memorizing mathematical equations or formulas nor does he or she need to memorize the dictionary. At the beginning of the math section, your student will find a box that has important formulas. In the vocabulary section, students are generally required to provide a word based on the context of the sentence. Many of the reading comprehension questions ask students to infer or to figure out what the author's purpose is. As such, if your student isn't used to thinking in this critical way, it may be difficult to prepare in short order. Some schools give practice SATs to students as early as the eighth grade to expose them to the style of SAT questions. You should follow suit and expose your student to the exam as soon as possible.

On the current SAT, test-takers are penalized for wrong answers (this will change on the redesigned SAT). Each wrong answer results in ¼ of a point reduction in your student's raw score for each section. Guessing isn't encouraged unless a student can narrow down the answer choices to two strong possibilities and make an educated guess from there. Otherwise, the question should be left blank, so that no points are deducted from your student's score. For more information on how the SAT is scored, check out sat.collegeboard. org/scores/how-sat-is-scored.

Your student's score report will also indicate how he or she fared against similarly situated students. When the score report mentions average scores, it is referring to the mean score of all students who took the most recent SAT of a particular graduating class. The percentiles on your student's score report are used to compare your student's scores to those of other students across the nation who will be graduating at the same time. For example, if your student's reading score is 500 and your state's percentile for a reading score of 500 is 47, this means your student did better than 47 percent of the state's college-bound seniors. The percentile portion of the report will show your student's percentile for total test-takers as well as test-takers within your state.

The Revised SAT®

Major changes are being made in the SAT test. If your child is planning to take the SAT after March 2016, they need to be aware of these changes. This will impact their preparation; for instance, if they take a practice test using the old-style test, or use an outdated test-prep book, they may be taken by surprise when the time comes to take the actual test. Here are some of the changes we know about at the time of this book's publication that could have a significant effect on how your student prepares:

1) **No penalty for wrong answers:** Woo-hoo—this is exciting! This has long been a complaint against the SAT, and it looks like the College Board finally got the message. So while students in the past have been told it's better to leave a blank rather than guess incorrectly on a question that has them stumped because it could hurt their score, now they need to know not to leave any question blank.

2) **Context:** The redesigned SAT will require students to interpret the meaning of a word through the context of the passage. This can be difficult for students who have been traditionally taught to memorize vocabulary definitions, because they may not truly understand what the words mean or how they are used. Using context clues requires the student to analyze the circumstances or facts (that is, the sentence or paragraph) in which the word is used in order to figure out the definition. The SAT's goal is to ensure that students have some level of mastery with the tested vocabulary. Studying those old lists of "500 Key SAT Words" won't be as useful as it used to be.

3) **Analyzing evidence:** The revised SAT will now be full of info-graphics and complex multi-paragraph passages, so students will have to do more than simply read the passages. They will need to interpret the passages to determine their answers and then pull text from the material to support their conclusions. Some questions will also require that students understand and analyze the structure of the passage or paragraph and correct both substance and grammar.

4) **Essay:** As in the past, the new essay will have a prompt and a passage. The new essay prompt will be released in advance and stay consistent from test to test, but the source material for the passage will change from test to test. Students will have to analyze the passage and explain how the author built the argument and then use evidence within that passage to support how the author reached that conclusion.

5) **Math:** The redesigned math sections of the SAT will now focus on problem solving and data analysis, algebra, and advanced math. Here is a summary of what the test may be covering:

- Problem solving and data analysis
  - Ratios
  - Percentages
  - Proportional reasoning
- Algebra
  - Linear equations and systems
- Advanced math
  - Familiarity with complex equations
  - Manipulation of complex equations

Finally, there will be changes in the way the test is scored. To better understand the changes in the SAT and how it will be scored starting in 2016, check the College Board website regularly for updates (https://www.collegeboard.org/delivering-opportunity/sat/redesign).

The ACT®

The ACT is a college-readiness assessment test created in 1959 by Everett Franklin Lindquist. The test was intended to be a competitor to the College Board's SAT. In 2005, an optional writing test was added to the ACT—at the same time the SAT made a similar change.

The ACT is said to be most similar to tests your student currently takes in school because it is more content-based. You either know the math or you don't. There is no formula or diagram key at the beginning of the math section, as appears in the SAT. In addition, I would argue that the test is more of an endurance test than the SAT. The ACT's first section, English, has 75

Key Info About the ACT®

Test dates: September, October, December, February, April

Duration: English (75 questions in 45 minutes); math (60 questions in 60 minutes); reading (40 questions in 35 minutes); science (40 questions in 35 minutes); and writing (one prompt, 30 minutes)

Sections: English, math, reading, science, writing (optional)

Score: range of 1–36 for each section

Cost: $36.50 (without writing) and $52.50 (with writing)

questions that must be answered in 45 minutes. The SAT's sections only last about 25 minutes apiece.

The ACT test has its advantages and disadvantages. Like the SAT, the ACT also compares your student's score to others' scores through ranks. Unlike the SAT, the ACT only counts the questions your student answered correctly towards his or her raw score, and does not deduct points for incorrect answers.

The national ranks tell you how your student's scores compare to those of the most recent graduates who took the ACT. The numbers indicate the cumulative percentage of students who scored at or below a given score. They provide a detailed analysis of whether or not your student is considered college-ready based on the scores in each content section.

So Which Test Does My Child Need to Take?

SAT, ACT, or both? That's the question that perplexes many high school juniors. If the colleges where they want to apply require a specific test, then it's an easy decision. But the number of schools that accept only the SAT or only the ACT is declining, and most colleges today accept scores from either test. A few schools are even test-optional, meaning they don't require applicants to submit scores from either test. Some students choose to take both tests, and then they submit the scores that are stronger. But others prefer to focus their preparation time, effort, and funds on just one test.

If your student is applying to schools that accept both tests, how do you decide *which* test they should direct their effort toward? They could give each test a try and see how well they perform. Ask your guidance counselor for practice tests for both the ACT and SAT. Have your student take the practice tests, grade both, and see which one has the better score. Ask your student which they felt most comfortable with, and check to see if that comfort level was reflected in their score. If there is a clear difference in scores or if the scores are similar but your child feels more comfortable with one test over the other, it's probably best to focus their test-preparation efforts on that test.

Even though the changes being made to the SAT are said to make it more like the ACT, they are still two totally different tests. As such, the strategies used to prepare for one test may not be as useful when preparing for the other. It's easy to state the differences between the two tests, but it's not so easy to study differently for each one. The ACT is a content- or achievement-based test that evaluates what the student learned in school, rather than skills or abilities. The SAT is more of a skills-based test, which measures both verbal and reasoning abilities. Because of these differences, if your student plans or needs to take both tests, I would strongly recommend that he or she studies for one test at a time. Your student needs to work toward performing well in the game.

ESTABLISH A BASELINE. In order for you to figure out how your student will perform in the game, there has to be a scrimmage. You need to put your child on the field for a simulated exam, under real exam conditions, and in the morning, so that the practice is as close to the real game as it can get. A practice test will help you figure out how much help your child really needs so that you aren't wasting money and time. What are the areas in which your child needs improvement? Does your child need subject-specific help or help with pacing?

Test your child's skill competencies by having your student take a timed practice test. In most cases, you can get old standardized tests with a scorecard for free or a small charge. Both the SAT (http://sat.collegeboard.org/practice/sat-practice-test) and the ACT (http://www.actstudent.org/sampletest/) offer free access to previous editions of their tests. Have your child take one of these tests.

Since standardized tests are timed, the best way to conquer them is to have a good handle on basic test-taking ability. The better your child's skill competency, the better your child's score should be. But if it isn't, there are additional variables to consider.

Kaye, one of my brightest students, had a huge case of test anxiety. When she and I worked through problems, one-on-one and untimed, she got almost every problem on the ACT correct. Yet, under timed conditions, she froze. She couldn't focus and second-guessed herself on each and every question. It showed on her score report.

Sometimes, it isn't just about being able to do the math. With Kaye, we were able to focus our efforts on test-taking skills since her problem area wasn't the content. We worked on managing her stress, pacing through the exam, becoming comfortable attacking the test questions in 'strength order' rather than in the order they appeared on the test, and timing each section through the exam. Kaye took a practice test each time we met, applied the various techniques she learned, and eventually became competent at managing her test anxiety. Figuring out your child's strengths and weaknesses before getting help with test prep will go a long way toward finding the right kind of help.

DETERMINE WHAT CORRECTIONS TO MAKE. If your child takes the practice exam through one of the websites previously listed, each will give you recommendations as well as provide a detailed breakdown of your student's score immediately upon completing the exam. If you pay for your child to take one of the official ACT or SAT tests administered at your school or another location, you will receive a similarly detailed report, either via e-mail or a letter. Finally, if your student takes the test from a test-prep book, you or your student will have to manually grade the practice test and examine the results.

The goal is to figure out where your student falls short. If your student is scoring well on all sections of the ACT except for English, you might decide to find a study course or create a study plan that emphasizes the skills tested in that section. The scored exam will also give you a sense of how well a student performs on various sections, which can help determine whether the student should pursue a broad or focused style of prep course. For example, if a student has a respectable score on all sections except math, then he or she might decide to find a study course that emphasizes only math. If the student needs help in each of the test subjects, she would find a general prep course to enroll in.

DETERMINE THE TYPE OF HELP YOUR STUDENT NEEDS. To find the right assistance for your child, you have to know your child. Here is a good example.

> *Ashley is one of the best parents I've ever worked with. I met Ashley in a bookstore—I was picking up some additional resources for my private school students, and Ashley was looking for an ACT-prep book for her daughter. I suggested some books that worked for my students, and Ashley asked for one of my business cards. I thought nothing of it and was happy to help.*
>
> *Almost a year later, I got a call. Ashley's daughter had taken the ACT once and didn't score as high as she had hoped. Ashley knew her daughter was quiet, and she worried that in a large test-prep class, her daughter wouldn't speak up or ask for help. We created a test-prep program that allowed her daughter to benefit from in-class discussion without the pressure of being in the room with 20 other students. Ashley reached out to two other parents who had students who needed help prepping for the ACT and formed a small tutoring group.*

Individual tutoring can be valuable for students who need one-on-one attention and a customized study plan to meet their needs. However, these sessions can also be intense, creating more stress than accountability for some students. They might feel more comfortable in a small group or classroom setting that allows them to blend in with other students.

In addition, many students are able to feed off of each other in small group and classroom settings. Your student may benefit from hearing from other students and discovering that they have the same struggles as the other students in the class.

At the end of the day, you know your child better than anyone else. Test preparation gives you the opportunity for you to place your child in the best possible position. The only way your child is going to get the hang of testing is if he or she is taught how to conquer the test in an environment that fits. Trust me, once you are clear about the best way your student learns, you will be able to find courses, tutors, books, and websites that are within your budget and that get the job done.

DETERMINE YOUR BUDGET. Prices for test-prep courses can range from free to thousands of dollars. After you have determined that your student needs help, you need to figure out how much you can spend to help him or her prepare for these exams. Compare the options. Ask how many instruction hours are offered, how many practice tests the student will take, and whether the program has a guarantee. Also, find out if books or other educational materials are included in the cost of the course or have to be bought separately. There is a list of some major test-prep providers in the Resources chapter of this book.

Here's the Test Plan for Junior Year

Fall

In October, your child needs to take the PSAT/NMSQT. Your student can ask their guidance counselor or research online to find out when and where this test (and all the subsequent tests) will be given and what they need to do to register. Dates for this and all standardized tests are the same nationally and are set and publicized months in advance. The benefits of taking this exam are twofold. First, this test is preparation for the SAT. Secondly, just taking the test puts your child in the running for a National Merit Scholarship.

Next, it's a matter of determining which other tests your student should take and when. The SAT is usually given seven times during an academic year while the ACT is given six times.

If your student feels ready, he or she could also register for and take the SAT in December. Your student will have the month of November to take a couple practice tests before the real thing in December.

But if they're not ready that soon for the SAT, then, after the PSAT/NMSQT, it's time to transition and register to take the ACT in February.

Winter

By December, you should have received your student's PSAT/NMSQT results. Students who scored extremely high will be notified that they are going to the next round of the National Merit Scholarship competition and will be given instructions on additional information to submit. The PSAT/NMSQT score report also comes with a free SAT study plan that outlines your student's strengths and weaknesses. This customized plan can help him or her work on areas that need improvement.

However, if you registered your student to take the February ACT, have your student hold off working on this SAT study plan until after he or she takes the ACT. As mentioned in the previous section, the study strategies for the two tests are quite different. Working on strengthening your student's reasoning and verbal skills for the SAT may take a bit more time than memorizing math formulas and grammar rules for the ACT.

There are different schools of thought on which tests to take and when to take them. Taking the SAT as soon as possible after the PSAT/NMSQT may be beneficial, since the content and format of the tests is similar and will be fresh in the student's mind. Then there's a two-month gap and winter break between the December SAT and the February ACT, which would allow the student time to shift their focus and prepare for the different test. But each student's situation will be different: some students may only be taking the PSAT/NMSQT and ACT, others may have particularly challenging semester exams to prepare for or research papers to write, a family vacation over winter break may cut into prep time, the test date may conflict with another obligation, and so on. What's most important is making sure your child prepares and then takes the test they need to take as soon as they possibly can, so there is time to do additional prep and take the tests again if necessary. Your student's guidance counselor may also have some advice and insights specific to your student.

Finally, many colleges require SAT Subject Tests™ for certain majors. If your student has determined his or her major now, you may want to discuss with your student's guidance counselor whether your son or daughter should take any of the SAT Subject Tests. If you're not familiar with these tests, they're hour-long, content-based tests in the following subjects: literature, U.S. History, world history, math–level 1, math–level 2, biology, chemistry, physics, French, French with listening, German, German with listening, Spanish, Spanish with listening, modern Hebrew, Italian, Latin, Chinese with listening, Japanese with listening, and Korean with listening. Some schools use the scores to place students in appropriate-level courses; at other colleges/universities, students may receive credit for introductory-level courses, based on their SAT Subject Test™ score.

Spring

If they haven't already done so, your student should contact the admissions offices of the colleges he or she is interested in to find out which SAT Subject Tests are required, if any. In addition, your child should also find out if these schools require the Writing Section of the SAT or ACT. Then, have your student take the SAT, the SAT Subject Tests, and/or the ACT during the spring semester. Even though it might seem easier to get all the tests over with at once, it's probably a good idea to avoid taking the SAT and the SAT Subject Test(s) on the same day, if possible.

If you plan to have your student take a prep course during the spring semester, he or she should register for a late spring or early summer ACT and/or SAT (check dates as they change each calendar year).

Even though the tests are administered again in the fall, those should be the absolute last times your student takes the ACT or SAT before applying for college. Ideally, your child's scores in the spring semester will be strong enough so that he or she can spend senior year focusing on applying to college and getting financial aid in order, rather than retaking the SAT or ACT. But it's good to know it's possible to take the tests again in the fall, so your student can spend more time preparing over the summer if necessary.

Moving Beyond Testing— What's Next?

It's taken awhile to get here, but let's go back to our earlier football analogy. By the end of junior year, your student has gone to the film room, reviewed the tape, lifted some weights, undergone conditioning, made corrections, and played in the game. At this point, students should be able to visualize themselves on a college campus, so now the search should become more tangible. Look at the schools on your child's list, and start making arrangements for some college visits, if you haven't done so already.

Of course, your child doesn't have to wait until after taking the SAT or ACT tests in order to start visiting colleges—some schools start reaching out to juniors with special visit days already in the fall. But the second semester of the junior year, particularly over spring break, is traditionally when families start the visit process in earnest, although many later admit they wish they had started earlier. Sometimes visiting a campus can help motivate students as they prepare for tests and research majors. From that standpoint, it can be helpful to just go and visit a college that may be nearby, even if the school isn't necessarily on the student's list. Every college's website lists its visit schedule, and unless it's a day specifically for students who've already been admitted, high school students at all grade levels are usually welcome.

Choosing Your College/University

There are so many factors that go into choosing a college. Some of it may depend on the limitations and guidelines that you have to set. For example, my mother wanted me to go to Oakwood University in Huntsville, Alabama. I did not want to go there, but she made an offer that I couldn't refuse: Go to Oakwood and she would pay my tuition. So, to Oakwood I went, kicking and screaming. It ended up being one of the best decisions of my life. Choosing a college was easy for us because we had one school in mind from the start. But for most families, it isn't that simple.

You and your student are going to have to narrow your large list down to a few schools, schedule some visits to see what you think about the various campuses, ask the right questions, and come to a final decision. I will give you some points to consider that can help you get your list down to a manageable size. Take the list of schools that your student is interested in, and score each one on a scale from 1 to 5 in each of the following categories (1 = terrible and 5 = excellent).

College Fairs and College Representative Visits

College fairs are often the perfect way to get started. These are formal gatherings that allow students to meet many college admission representatives in one setting. Sometimes a large high school will host its own fair; other times these fairs may be held in a nearby city in a large meeting room or auditorium. There are usually dozens of colleges represented with personnel and materials. Students are able to browse around, chat casually with the admission representatives, and gather information about course offerings, tuition, application requirements, college life, and much more.

Your child's guidance counselor should be able to let you know what opportunities are available in your area. Your student should be able to see a list of the participating schools in advance. You should go through that list with your student in advance, and determine which schools are "must-sees" for them by the end of the college fair. It can be a bit overwhelming for some students, so be prepared if your student announces they're ready to go home after just a short time there. At the very least, your student will probably come home with a variety of brochures and give-away items from numerous colleges and universities.

Depending on the size of your student's school, representatives from various colleges and universities may also visit there on a regular basis. Again, your student's guidance counselor is the person who will know which schools are visiting and when. If there is a representative coming from a school your student is even a little bit interested in, your student needs to let their counselor know so the counselor can make arrangements for your student to meet with that representative one on one, if possible.

School Size—Determining What's Best for Your Student

In college, the issue of class size goes to an entirely new level. Some freshman classes can have hundreds of students in them. In classrooms that size, your student will be fighting for attention— while the smaller the class size, the more attention your student will likely get. When I was in college, I had 40 students in my freshman English class. My teacher knew my name and when I was (or wasn't) in class. She knew my work and when I was slacking. My professor knew me enough to call me out if my work or class participation was substandard. There will always be stellar professors like this one who remember every student's name, know when a student is absent, and check in when he or she isn't doing so well. However, on big campuses that kind of small-school intimacy can be lost.

In addition, while the college academic environment is vastly different from high school, in that college students bear the burden of keeping pace and taking charge of their own education, large class sizes of 100 or more students can make it extremely difficult for students to get their questions answered and receive the attention they may need on an individual level. At larger colleges, students will likely have to break out of their shells and be go-getters in order to get additional help from professors, as well as simply to be seen and heard in class. That isn't a necessarily bad thing. Students need to learn to be proactive, be bold and assertive when needed, and get their needs met.

It goes back to what we have discussed previously. You know your student. If your child has been a bit sheltered (I was) and needs a bit more time to grow up before being thrown into the real world, a small school may provide the cushion he or she needs (which is why Oakwood was just right for me). Talk to your child about it. See what they think, and put a check mark by the schools that fit their ideal. Then, move on down the list to the rest of the topics.

Student Interaction

Smaller colleges can feel like high school, and I don't mean that in a negative way. It can feel like high school because of the size, which makes it easier for students to get to know others on campus. That can be a wonderful thing and an annoying thing, depending on your student's preferences and perspective.

On a large campus, it may be difficult to get to know other students, especially until a year or two into school when your child will connect with other students in the same major. For example, students who attended the University of Michigan in 2013 were on campus with 43,710 students. On a campus that size, your child will see the students in their major more frequently because they will end up taking the many of the same classes together—and even that's not a given if your child's major is one that attracts hundreds of students. In order to get to know people outside of that group, your student will need to be involved in other activities. That's why extracurricular activities are a good way to offset some of the departmental isolation that can occur.

Extracurricular Activities

Let's define extracurricular to be everything outside of your student's academic career. This includes sports, clubs, internships, and everything else! I'd say the point to extracurricular activities in college is to gain experience, develop skills, expand awareness, and do what you love. If your student's career path or course of study provides opportunities to work in a lab or an apprenticeship, he or she should definitely take advantage of this in college.

The college your student selects should provide an avenue for your student to explore their interests and possible career field. If your student wants to be a writer, make sure the college has a school newspaper or literary magazine that your student can work for and gain real world experience. Employers will look for this kind of experience when hiring college graduates. Don't get me wrong, employers like a student with a solid GPA, but in this competitive job market, experience will help your future college graduate stand out.

But just as at the high school level, extracurricular activities in college don't necessarily have to be career-related. Colleges today offer hundreds of clubs and groups that students can join—many of them created and run by the students. Taking part in activities outside of class can help students build relationships, learn new skills, grow as a person, relieve stress, open their eyes to majors or career possibilities they may not have considered, and just plain have fun! Students might want to continue activities they did in high school; while they may not be able to play their sport at a Division I level, they can still enjoy being part of an intramural team. Forensics, debate, quiz bowl, and other academic pursuits allow students to travel to competitions on other college campuses. Service groups connect students with the community beyond the campus borders. And special-interest groups allow them to bond with like-minded students as they explore a broad range of matters, from faith and environmental interests to animal welfare and gender/sexuality issues. The Greek system is also an important factor for many students (no, it's nothing like *Animal House*!). As your child evaluates colleges, have them review each school's list of extracurricular offerings and consider which ones might spark an interest.

Name Recognition

For certain career paths, the college your student goes to will matter. Advantages to attending a school with name recognition are the connections students will make, the professors they will learn from, the people they will rub elbows with, and the school's alumni network, to name just a few.

Different schools have different levels of name recognition, and that is not necessarily dependent upon the size of the college. Ivy League schools, for example, clearly have name recognition, outstanding applicants, and some of the strongest alumni networks in the world. It all depends on what your student is looking for and what would be a good fit as he or she later attempts to build a life and career.

Keep in mind, however, that employers and graduate schools also look for outstanding skills and experience, no matter what school your student attends. College pedigree matters in certain places, certain businesses, and to a certain set of people. It doesn't matter what college your son attended if he gets a job and doesn't know what he is doing. It may be best to go for the school that will give your child the skills he or she needs to be successful and will provide an environment in which to thrive.

Other Factors to Consider

Housing: Is your child going to need to live on campus in a residence hall? I am an only child, and I absolutely hated having a roommate in college. However, the college I attended had a strict rule that required all freshmen to live in the dorm on campus with a curfew. Bummer for me, but my mom loved it, so away I went to endure a disciplined freshman year. You and your student need to learn about the housing options for the colleges your student is considering. Does the school require students to live on campus for a particular length of time? What type of housing options are available—there is a lot more variety than there used to be, from basic dormitories, to suite-style units, to on-campus apartments. If students live on campus, are they also required to purchase a meal plan? If the school allows students to live off-campus, explore the cost and availability of housing in that particular community, keeping in mind that there are additional expenses associated with furnishing a student apartment and having students purchase all their own groceries and meals. Or if you choose a college in or near the city where you live, can your student continue to live at home and commute to the campus? What are your student's feelings about this?

Facilities: It may seem unimaginable to you now, but believe me when I say the library will become your student's regular hangout in college. It's so important to check out the library, labs, and other facilities at the colleges your student wants to attend. Must-haves vary from major to major. But bear in mind that if your daughter wants to major in music production and engineering, the school she chooses should have state-of-the-art equipment and production capabilities. If your son wants to major in biochemical engineering, the school needs to have the facilities necessary to teach him how to grow plant, animal, and microbial cells in bioreactors and to separate their products, and so on. You get the picture.

Distinguished Faculty: Being around genius can rub off. For that reason alone, you should research the faculty. For example, Emory University has an amazing faculty roster. Emory's faculty includes:

- Former U.S. President Jimmy Carter
- His Holiness the XIV Dalai Lama
- CNN's chief medical correspondent Dr. Sanjay Gupta
- Pulitzer Prize–winning author Hank Klibanoff
- Former Director of the U.S. Centers for Disease Control and Prevention Jeffrey Koplan
- Booker Prize–winning novelist Sir Salman Rushdie

- Pulitzer Prize–winning poet Natasha Trethewey, 19th U.S. Poet Laureate

When I was applying to law school, one of the things that helped narrow down my list of potential schools was the faculty members, even though they weren't recognizable names and I didn't personally know who they were. No, I was attracted to the faculty because each one of them had been practicing attorneys before they decided to become law professors. I knew that when I was in my criminal law class, I was learning from someone who was able to provide real-world insight into trying a murder case as opposed to theory. That was extremely important for me as a law student. Even if I didn't end up practicing law in that particular area, it was essential for me to have learned from people with real-world experience in my areas of interest.

Any school your student plans to apply to should be able to detail the accomplishments of its faculty. While it may not matter to a student majoring in chemistry that Jimmy Carter is a professor at Emory, it may matter that the chemistry professor has been doing cancer research for the past twenty-five years. A rich and diverse faculty with a range of experience and expertise can add value to the student experience on campus.

Geography: How near or far away does your student want to be, and how far away do *you* want your child to be? Factor in the expense of travel to and from school, whether your student plans to commute or fly halfway across the country. If it's an airplane ride, are direct flights available? If it's only accessible by car, how will your student get home on breaks? Will you be willing to spring for a plane ticket if your child gets homesick and wants to come home for a weekend? How hard is it to get there?

Climate: Will your beach-loving kid be able to handle a Minnesota winter? Or does your New Englander want to experience something completely different and try the California lifestyle? Will your student need to buy an entirely new wardrobe to accommodate attending a school in a different part of the country?

Graduation/Transfer Rate: How many students start, but don't finish? How many start here but transfer somewhere else? How many students finish in four years?

Support Services: What does the school offer in terms of student services, start to finish? How does a particular school make sure freshmen don't flunk out or slip between the cracks? How strong is the career services department, and when do the career counselors start working with students—senior year or before?

Campus Amenities: Little things can make a big difference in student happiness/success. Does the student union serve great chai (your student's favorite), or does your child have to hitch a ride into town to find the nearest cool coffee shop? Are there fitness classes and exercise facilities available for all students or just athletes?

Town and Gown: Look beyond the campus boundaries. What does the surrounding community have to offer in terms of internships, career possibilities, community service and involvement, recreation, shopping, activities, and so on? Is it a safe community? Is it urban, suburban, or rural? What are the transportation options? Is the college a well-respected or reviled part of the community?

Safe, Match, and Reach Schools

After you've evaluated each school on your list of possibilities in these areas, take the list and break it down into three categories: safe, match, and reach.

SAFE colleges are those that your child has an excellent chance of being accepted to and are affordable for your family. The colleges in this category should be schools your student would be okay with attending, even if they're not his or her first choice. Think of how the school will view your applicant. Will the admissions representative find your student to be a below average, average, or above average applicant? What are your student's chances for financial aid and scholarships at these colleges?

MATCH schools are just that—the colleges that are good matches for your student overall. While the safe colleges may not have everything your student needs, the good matches are a great fit. Your student should be a competitive applicant at the good match schools.

REACH schools are highly selective schools that—because of their reputation and high standards—are probably in the reach category for just about every student. Certainly your student can apply to a reach school, but that choice should be realistic enough to be worth the effort and cost of applying. Don't suggest that your son apply to Yale just for the sake of applying when he isn't close to making the cut there. You also have to consider what happens if your student does get accepted by a reach school. Sure, it would be awesome, but can your family afford the tuition? Make sure that, even when applying to reach schools, your student's test scores and GPA are clearly in the top 25 percent of the applicant pool.

Are Your Categories Balanced?

Now that you and your student have scored and categorized the schools you're considering, you need to make sure you haven't gotten carried away in any particular category. For instance, if you have more than three reach schools, you might be reaching a bit too far. Keep *reach* to one or two schools. Reach schools are the dream schools, but they may not be the schools at which your child is realistically competitive in the applicant pool. Ideally, the bulk of your student's school selections should be in the *match* category. You should have at least two *safe* schools.

And don't have too many schools. Is it realistic to research, visit, and submit applications to a dozen colleges? When it comes time to make a decision, will the details of all those schools blur together? Even going through the process with six schools—two in each category—can be a big undertaking. This may be the time to make some cuts.

These are just a few things to consider when you narrow down your child's college list. If you scored each school using the criteria listed earlier, it may be time to remove some of those schools that have a lower score. Once you eliminate those that don't measure up, start planning your college visits.

College Visits

Once your list is solid, it's time to start seriously visiting these schools (if you haven't already). Before your student reaches out to the admissions department, have them write down reasons why they want to go to each particular school. Chances are someone from the school (or eventually the school's application) will ask your student why they want to attend that school. It's better to have a well-reasoned response prepared prior to any conversations with a college representative.

Scheduling Your Time on Campus

College visits are important. Seeing the campus, speaking to students, or meeting professors and administrators will help your student to determine if he or she really wants to go to that school. It's that intangible quality called "fit." I visited schools, but nothing felt like Oakwood did, even though I claimed I didn't want to be there. I'll never forget the feeling I had when I stepped onto that campus. Over time, I knew that I was supposed to be there. Clarity comes through action. These campus visits may be just what your child needs.

You and your student should check the college's website and find out when you can visit. Does the college have a certain weekend open house coming up soon? Maybe you've already been receiving materials through mail and e-mail from this school—don't pass up an opportunity to go on a specified visit day, even if your student hasn't finished taking SATs or ACTs or hasn't narrowed down their list this far yet. If there aren't any specified events, then schedule your own visit. Make sure your student is prepared with questions for the admission department representative he or she may have an opportunity to meet. Great questions refer to those things your student wasn't able to determine after looking on the school's website or through any brochures. This will demonstrate interest in the school and can help make your student memorable.

PREPARING FOR THE VISIT. You don't have to visit each and every college on your child's target list. But you and your child should try to visit as many of their top schools as time and geography allow. Words and pictures in a brochure or on the website can only convey so much. Your child may be spending four years on that campus. Checking it out in person can turn a school he or she is lukewarm about into a top contender—or it can work the other way, too.

Before you go to each school, there are many things to consider. Are there any deal breakers? Are there any must haves? Is your child interested in a particular major or program? Is your student prepared to be interviewed by an admission counselor as part of the visit? Do you have questions for an admission or financial aid counselor?

Think about places on campus that you would like to see or places that are essential to college life. For example, the library at my college left much to be desired. My major required a lot of research and writing, and I knew I would be spending a large amount of time in the library. So after visiting the college, I became aware that I would have to find a way to resolve the library issue. However, there were several other things about the school that outweighed the library. Think about the kinds of things that will make college life work for your student, and ask whether or not the college has those things—whether it's state-of-the-art labs for your biology student or a student-run TV station for your budding broadcast journalist.

In order to make the most of your college visit, have your list of questions, deal breakers, must haves, and places to visit prepared before visiting the campus. Hopefully, many of the questions will be answered during the tour. If not, you should be able to have your questions answered by someone in the admission office.

WHAT TO EXPECT ON YOUR VISIT. Depending on the size of the college or university, you can expect the admission office to offer daily tours, group tours, and/or special open house or visit day programs.

Daily tours are typically conducted one-on-one or in a small group, and you can also expect individual time with an admissions counselor, faculty member, or current student. You and your child will be taken on a tour of the campus, which will probably include the library, dining hall, dorms, gym or auditorium, classrooms, student services, and other facilities. If your student requests it, he or she may even have the opportunity to sit through an actual class. Group tours will be similar to the daily tours, but typically have between 10 to 50 people. With groups of this size, it may be difficult to ask individual questions. Whether individual or in a group, tours are often given by current students. Be sure to ask questions—the student perspective and insights are often refreshingly honest.

An open house or visit day will be more structured and offer more than just a tour. These events are open to all prospective students, and they often last a large part of the day. Students and parents can attend informational sessions that cover a variety of topics presented by administrators, faculty members, and sometimes even students: what the college has to offer, the admission process, financial aid, what kinds of things are there to do on campus, study-abroad programs, and so on. Some schools even have alumni come back and discuss their experiences with attendees. While you probably won't have the opportunity to sit in a class as part of an event like this, you may be given the opportunity to speak with a professor. There will certainly be a tour, and your student may even get to have a meal in the college's dining hall.

Keep in mind that college visits are the college's sales pitch. Ask lots of questions and remember things that stand out or that may be glossed over. If you want information outside of the sales pitch, you may want your student to have an informal conversation with a current student during your visit. Take notes and talk with your student after each campus visit; listen to what they liked and didn't like before sharing your impressions.

Questions to Ask the Admissions Officer on Your College Visit

An admission interview is more than just a representative of the college asking your student personal questions. This representative will also be watching to see what questions your student asks of him or her—it demonstrates inquisitiveness and your student's genuine interest in the school. So if your student has an opportunity to meet with a college admission officer, he or she should definitely take advantage of the opportunity to ask some meaningful questions. It's important to ask the right questions. If you can find the answer in a quick perusal of the college's website—that's a question you do not want to ask. For example, here are some questions NOT to ask the admission department representative:

- How many students attend your school?
- Does the school offer a major in XYZ?
- Am I required to live on campus during my freshman year?
- Is there a women's volleyball team here?
- What is the application deadline? Does the school offer early decision or early action?

Asking those kinds of questions shows the admission officer that your student hasn't done his or her homework about the school. Again, if the answer's on the school's website—don't ask the question!

What are some questions that your student should ask? Here are a few good examples:

- I'm very interested in sustainable food and organic gardening, but I didn't see that listed on the website among the current available clubs. Would it be possible for me to initiate a food security club at your college/university? What steps would I need to take to start a new club?
- I saw on the website that the college/university offers a self-designed major. I might be interested in this and am interested

in examples of self-designed majors that other students have designed? Would it be possible to use the self-designed major to combine my interests in nutrition, economic development, and city planning?

- I read that first-year students participate in service-learning projects, but I didn't see a list of the projects that this year's freshmen took part in. Would you please tell me the types of service-learning or community service opportunities?

- If I major in nutrition, will there be any opportunities for me to have an internship or to work with a professor on research?

- The study-abroad program in Brazil looks interesting. When do students usually take part in programs like this and does it impede them from graduating in four years?

- Are there any special programs for freshmen beyond orientation to help them successfully make the transition to college and navigate the first year?

- Aside from the amazing things noted on the college/university's website and brochures, what would you say is its most outstanding feature?

After you have visited some campuses, your list and ranking of schools will probably change—it's eye-opening how different a college can be when you visit in person versus photos on the website or in a brochure. The next steps are important: you and your student can begin reviewing the various applications for each school, planning what your student is going to write about in their application essay, and making a list of recommenders.

Next Steps

The next steps your student should work on are the materials associated with the college/university application(s): essays, letters of recommendation, and the actual application. These are things your child should start working on during the summer after their junior year. You can find detailed information about this in **Chapter 4— Senior Year: It All Comes Down To This!** Look ahead and check it out!

JUNIOR YEAR CHECKLIST

Questions to Answer before Senior Year

FALL:

☐ Has your student created an e-mail account specifically for college correspondence yet? If not, they should. Make sure the address created is simple and professional—not *GamerDude4ever* or *luvs2shop.*

☐ Did your child take the PSAT/NMSQT in October?

☐ Did you receive the PSAT/NMSQT score report?

☐ If your child qualified to advance in the NMSQT competition, did he or she submit the additional information requested?

☐ Did you review the PSAT/NMSQT score report for strengths and weaknesses in particular subjects?

☐ Did you and your child plan and decide when he or she would take the SAT and/or ACT? Has your student registered for those tests?

WINTER:

☐ Did you and your child begin narrowing down the list of colleges?

☐ Do any of the schools on that target list prefer one college entrance exam over the other?

☐ Does your student have a preference? ACT or SAT?

☐ Will your child be taking a test-prep course? Has he or she registered for that course?

☐ If not, did you purchase a test-prep book and create a schedule based on the timeline in the book?

☐ Did you sign up for any of the free test-prep resources outlined in this chapter?

☐ Did your child take the December SAT?

☐ Did you receive the SAT results with the detailed study plan?

☐ Did your child take a practice ACT over winter break?

☐ Did your student sit for the February ACT?

SPRING:

☐ Have you and your student evaluated and sorted the colleges on their list?

☐ Have you scheduled college visits at your student's safe, match, and reach schools?

☐ Have you started on the list of potential recommenders? Did all the teachers on that list teach your child within the previous two academic years?

☐ Did you pull all the essay prompts and questions from the application and/or websites from the colleges on your student's target list?

☐ Have you and your student created a calendar for all the upcoming deadlines? Remember to include other important dates on that calendar as well, such as midterms, AP exams, and finals, so you can plan accordingly.

☐ Did you create a file folder for each of the schools on your final list and a checklist for each school?

SUMMER:

☐ Have you spoken with the potential recommenders about whether they would write a letter for your student?

☐ Did you and your student visit the colleges on the list?

☐ Does your student have all the applications for each college?

☐ Do you have all the necessary deadlines outlined on your calendar and your child's calendar?

☐ Has your student completed one or two college essays and submitted them to a teacher or mentor for review?

☐ Are you ready for your student's senior year?

CHAPTER 4

Senior Year: It All Comes Down To This!

Suddenly it's here—senior year. How did those years of high school pass by so quickly? Your student's senior year is an exciting and nerve-wracking time, filled with dates, deadlines, and requirements to meet. On top of that are all the extra events and potential distractions, like prom, graduation parties, and those sentimental "lasts" like the last football game, last band concert, last pep rally, and so on. It's important to stay organized!

The first things you and your student need to keep track of are the deadlines, whether they're for visits, tests, college applications, financial aid, scholarships, and finally that big decision. Seems like a lot, right? Well, it is. The challenging news is that senior year could get extremely stressful for you and your student. The good news is that you'll make it. It all comes down to senior year. So let's get ready.

Hopefully, by the end of this chapter you will:

- Be able to guide your student toward the completion of their application essay(s).
- Help your student with the process of requesting and obtaining letters of recommendation.
- Ensure that all of your child's application materials are turned in on time.
- Make sure your student schedules, if applicable, their SAT®, ACT, AP®, I.B., and/or SAT Subject Test™(s) on time.
- Stay organized so you can help your student stay on track throughout the college admission process.
- Be prepared for the ups and downs of senior year.

Finish Strong: The Senior Year Schedule

Just as in your student's junior year, advance planning and marking everything on the calendar are important components to help you both stay on track. Here's a rundown of some of the major milestones during this academic year:

August/September

- Register for the ACT and/or SAT, if necessary. By *necessary,* I mean if your child hasn't yet taken one or both of these tests, or if their scores aren't as high as they need to be.
- Determine which colleges your student will be applying to.
- Schedule visits ASAP if you haven't finished visiting those colleges. Many schools have special visit days scheduled in the fall, just for seniors.
- Take stock of all the college application requirements:
  - What documents need to be compiled for each college's complete application?
  - What are the application deadlines for each college?
  - What are the deadlines for financial aid and scholarships?
  - Create ticklers (calendar reminders or computer pop-ups that nag you until you get something done) to remind you of the important due dates.
- Remind your student to make an appointment with the guidance counselor to make sure he or she is on track for graduation.
- Determine which, if any, SAT Subject Tests must be taken.
- Make sure your student's application essays are undergoing their final revisions.

October/November

- Make sure your student is meeting application deadlines, especially if he or she intends to apply early decision or early action.
- Request application fee waivers, if applicable.
- Request transcripts from the high school; your student needs to provide information on where they need to be sent.
- Verify that your student's ACT/SAT test scores have been sent to the selected colleges.
- Be sure your student has scheduled any I.B. exams (November registration deadline).
- Check online for the FAFSA (Free Application for Federal Student Aid) forms for the coming academic year. You cannot submit the form until after January 1, but you need to become familiar with the application and the documents and information you need to complete it.

December

- Make sure your student has their applications organized and ready to go prior to the deadlines for the regular-decision applications that will be due during the next two months.
- Get ready for your student to hear about any early decision or early action decisions.

January/February

- Complete and file the FAFSA application as soon as possible after January 1.
- Verify that your student's first-semester transcripts were sent to all the necessary colleges.
- Determine if it's necessary for your student to take the last accepted administration of the ACT and/or SAT for this college application cycle.

- Be on the lookout (with your student, of course) for any college admission decisions arriving via e-mail and/or snail mail.

March/April

- Be sure your student schedules any AP exams in March.
- Remind your student to check his or her e-mail inbox and home mailbox for responses from the colleges.
- Start comparing the financial aid packages that should be arriving from the schools where your student has been accepted.
- Schedule revisits to any colleges where your child has been accepted, if necessary, to help your student make a final decision. Some colleges offer "Accepted Student Days" when students can see the campus again, perhaps stay overnight, and meet with students and instructors.
- Help your student make the final decision of which college to attend.

May

- Send the commitment and deposit by the college's deadline.
- Follow all financial aid instructions.
- Request a final transcript and be sure that any AP/I.B. scores will be sent to the college when they are received (usually during the summer).

Wow, that's a lot, isn't it? Don't worry—we'll break down many of these in detail here in this chapter.

AP® and I.B. Exams

Advanced Placement (AP) Exams

As mentioned earlier in this book, the Advanced Placement (AP) program was created by the College Board to give high school students access to college-level courses. AP exams are administered in May of each school year on a prescribed date and time that is uniform across the country (to prevent cheating). The exam consists of multiple-choice questions and a free response section in the form of an essay or a problem-solving question. Students can take AP exams as juniors or seniors. Students usually take AP exams in conjunction with an AP class they took as part of their school curriculum; however, there are some students who may choose to study independently to take AP exams and potentially earn college credit. Note that there is a fee for taking an AP exam.

The exam is graded on a 5-point scale: 5 is extremely well-qualified, 4 is well-qualified, 3 is qualified, 2 is possibly qualified, and 1 is no recommendation. These scores are sent to the student, his or her high school, and the student's specified colleges in July. Some colleges will award credit for AP classes, but it usually depends on the student's score on the exam (in most cases, a 3 or higher), not just whether the student completed the course. Check with the colleges on your child's target list to determine whether your child can receive credit for his or her AP courses.

International Baccalaureate (I.B.) Exams

As with the AP exams, I.B. exams are given at the conclusion of a particular course that the student has taken as part of their high school curriculum. They may not be taken independently of the course. The exams are given during the first three weeks of May, with each subject test being conducted on a prescribed day, which is uniform around the world. Students may take the exams as juniors or seniors, depending on which year they took the course. Some of the courses and subsequent exams are termed "higher level" and cover two academic years' worth of material. The exams are usually essay-based or problem-based. There is a fee for taking any I.B. exam; students must register for the exams in the fall.

The exams are scored (on a 1 to 7 scale, with 7 being highest) and released to the student, their high school, and any colleges the student may have specified in early July. Each college usually has its own policies in place for awarding credit depending on the student's score on the exam.

Students can take I.B. exams in conjunction with only specific courses, or as part of an effort to earn the I.B. Full Diploma, which requires a full slate of exams and certain average on those exams, an extended essay, and other specific classes and projects.

Writing the Application Essay

At this point, your student is an excellent writer, right? Of course! Well, at least you hope so. However, writing a college application essay is quite different from any other writing your student had to do in high school. This essay isn't for a grade. Instead, it allows college admissions officers to get a peek at exactly who your student is and what his or her goals are, and it helps determine whether your student is a good fit for the school. Because this essay is an important part of the process, I would advise you to have your student start writing it early. By early, I mean during the summer before their senior year.

Look at the applications for the schools where your student plans to apply, and have your student begin writing drafts of responses to the essay prompts. Have someone credible review the essay drafts and provide critical feedback. While colleges may have similar questions, the essay prompts will probably not be the same across the board. If your student is applying to six colleges, you definitely don't want to wait until the week before the application is due for them to start writing their essays. The same rule applies to scholarship applications, which almost always require an essay, too.

Sample Questions

The Common Application is an online application service used by many schools to help streamline the application process. Students who are applying to more than one school that subscribes to The

Common Application (it will say so in the college's application information) can submit the Common Application once and the information in it will be shared with all the colleges to which your student wants to apply. However, many schools also have their own application supplement to the Common Application, often requiring—you guessed it—another essay question or two!

Just to provide you with a sample of the type of questions your child may have to choose from for their essay(s), here are the 2014–15 Common Application essay prompts. For that application year, the essay length was capped at 650 words.

The essay prompts are as follows:

> *Option #1: Some students have a background or story that is so central to their identity that they believe their application would be incomplete without it. If this sounds like you, then please share your story.*
>
> *Option #2: Recount an incident or time when you experienced failure. How did it affect you, and what lessons did you learn?*
>
> *Option #3: Reflect on a time when you challenged a belief or idea. What prompted you to act? Would you make the same decision again?*
>
> *Option #4: Describe a place or environment where you are perfectly content. What do you do or experience there, and why is it meaningful to you?*
>
> *Option #5: Discuss an accomplishment or event—formal or informal—that marked your transition from childhood to adulthood within your culture, community, or family.*

These prompts require your child to reflect. Great college essays are not easy to write. As you can see from the questions above, this kind of writing can be difficult for high school students. While they may feel comfortable writing about Shakespeare, the Spanish Inquisition, or DNA replication, writing about themselves and their feelings is challenging—there are no research sources or textbooks. Inspiration has to come from within and takes time to uncover. Your student should not wait until the fall of senior year to start thinking about their responses to questions like these. Your student will need time to write and will most certainly need time to edit.

In addition, your student should ask a teacher and/or mentor to review his or her essay and provide critical feedback. Applications are often cold documents that provide only the black and white of a student's background. The essay is an opportunity for those determining whether an applicant will be selected to hear your child's voice and find out who he or she really is, beyond their GPA and list of activities. Make sure your student spends the summer before senior year finding their voice and presenting it as best as possible to the colleges of their choice.

Recommendation Letters

I can't say this strongly enough: Students must not wait until the last minute to get their recommendation letters! In my mind, "last minute" means the fall semester of senior year—everyone asks for letters at that time. It is generally recommended that students should ask for letters of recommendation at least a month in advance of when they need them. I can agree with that, as long as your student's personal deadline for receiving the letter is at least two months before they are submitting the application. I say this knowing that your student will probably not get a recommendation that early. And you don't need just any recommendation—what you need is a great recommendation.

If you want great, you may have to give your recommenders some guidance and some time. For example, the Massachusetts Institute of Technology (MIT) has a section on its website that tells recommenders exactly what kind of letters they are looking for to help guide them in the decision-making process. MIT suggests that recommenders address some of the following questions:

- What is the context of your relationship with the applicant? If you do not know the applicant well and are only able to write a brief summary, please acknowledge this.

- Has the student demonstrated a willingness to take intellectual risks and go beyond the normal classroom experience?

- Does the applicant have any unusual competence, talent, or leadership abilities?

- What motivates this person? What excites him/her?

- How does the applicant interact with teachers? With peers? Describe his/her personality and social skills.

- What will you remember most about this person?

- If you have knowledge of MIT, what leads you to believe MIT is a good match for this person? How might he/she fit into the MIT community and grow from the MIT experience?

- Has the applicant ever experienced disappointment or failure? If so, how did he/she react?

- Are there any unusual family or community circumstances of which we should be aware?

After reading these questions, you can see that MIT isn't looking for letters that say "Jane is mature." Colleges want and value recommendation letters that reveal things about your student beyond grades and test scores. To get the kind of letter you need for your student, your best bet is to plan ahead and ask early.

Here are some tips to help guide you and your student through the process.

1) Get Organized:

- Find out how your student's high school handles teacher recommendations. Does the guidance office submit recommendations directly to the schools your student applied to along with transcripts? Will the teacher have to send the letter of recommendation directly to the college?

- Check to see how each college that your student is applying to wants to receive letters of recommendation and how many they require. Procedures and preferences vary.

- Start a file for each person from whom your student requests a recommendation letter. Keep a thank-you card in his or her file that your student can send when the recommendation has been sent. I'll share more about what else you need to include in the file.

2) **Create a List of Teachers:** A good letter of recommendation gives great insight about your student. The letter details their strengths and weaknesses as well as examples. As such, the teachers you and your student choose should be those who really know your student.

- Choose one core teacher—someone who teaches a core subject like English or math.

- As a secondary option you can also choose a coach or adviser for a school-based extracurricular activity. Again, this should be a teacher who knows your student's work, work ethic, and learning style and can shed a positive light on some of your student's strongest qualities.

- Consider the following when creating your list of teachers:
  – When did they teach your child? Ideally, you want someone who has taught your student within a two-year period.
  – What subject did they teach your child? Your student should find a math, science, English, social studies, and maybe foreign language teacher to write a letter of recommendation. An exception is if the school your student is applying to has specific guidelines or your child is pursuing a particular major, such as art or music, in which it is appropriate to have the teacher in that subject make the recommendation.
  – Think about the amount of time the teacher has taught high school. Your student should try to get a seasoned teacher to write the recommendation. If he or she is a newer

teacher, make sure the teacher has strong credentials. Sometimes schools ask for background information on the teacher. You don't want the recommendation to lose some of its weight because of a perceived lack of experience.

3) **Ask at the Right Time:** Be respectful and conscious of the teacher's time and responsibilities. At all costs, avoid requesting a letter of recommendation during the following times:

- Midterms

- Final exams

- First week of class

- Holidays or vacations

4) **Give Context and Information:** I previously mentioned creating a folder for each teacher your student will request a letter from. There should actually be two folders for each recommender: one that your student keeps for their records and one for the recommender with the necessary information about your student and the letter request. Keep a copy of everything you give the recommender in your student's file as well. Here's the information you should give a recommender:

- *Statement:* Have your student include in each request a statement of what he or she wants to do and why he or she wants to go to this particular college. It doesn't have to be a long, just a few-sentence summary.

- *Context:* Give the teacher some context and allow him or her to understand the importance of this letter. Include a list of all of the colleges your student is applying to, with addresses and application deadlines clearly stated. If you are applying to particular departments, scholarships, or other special programs, clarify that information for the teacher.

- *An addressed and stamped (if necessary) envelope:* This is so the completed letter can be sent to the college or high school guidance office.

- *Your student's contact information:* Name, phone number, and e-mail address— should the recommender have any questions or have problems completing the recommendation on time.

- *Talking points:* Just to be safe, I would include something similar to that MIT list shown earlier in this chapter. Check with the schools your student is applying to, and determine whether the school outlines what they want from a recommendation letter. If so, share that with the recommender.

- *Some background:* Provide the recommender with some information about your student and your family. There doesn't need to be a vast amount of detail, but enough. Let the teacher know how long your child has gone to the school, how long your family has lived in the community, how many siblings your student has, and so on. This will give the teacher some additional insight into your student's situation.

5) **How to Ask:** Your child should ask the teacher face to face, if possible. Your student should also ask the teacher if he or she would be comfortable writing the recommendation. If your student feels like the teacher isn't enthusiastic about recommending him or her, then your child should move on to the next possible recommender. If you have the opportunity to speak with a potential recommender, here are some things you should discuss:

- Talk about your student's class participation in class.

- Discuss specific work or projects your child has done.

- If there are problem areas in your student's transcript or high school history—like low scores freshman year because your family moved to a new city and your student had difficulty adjusting, for example—address it head-on, and mention it to the teacher at the meeting. Explain why the difficulty arose and how your student has overcome it.

6) **Follow Up:** If you haven't received confirmation that your student's letter of recommendation has been submitted, follow

up two weeks before your deadline with a gentle reminder. If it still hasn't been submitted, you may need to consider moving on to a back-up recommender. Once the letter is submitted, have your student send a thank-you note. People don't send handwritten notes enough anymore. It can go a long way, and it makes your student memorable, which could be useful later.

Finally, make sure to waive the right to review the recommendation letters. If you did your job up front, you won't need to review the letters later. Furthermore, I think it shows that you have faith in the teachers and in the reputation of your student if you allow the letters to be sent blindly. Keep in mind that schools vary in how much they rely on recommendation letters. Your child may not need a recommendation letter for the college application, but he or she may need to submit one later for a scholarship application. Be sure to let the recommender know whether the letter is for a scholarship or for a college application so that the recommender can tailor the letter accordingly.

Organization Is Key!

The key to staying sane throughout the application process is keeping up with deadlines and staying organized. I am a bundle of organized chaos, but that works (sometimes) for me. My mother, on the other hand, is the most organized individual I have ever seen. She still has files with my kindergarten art projects in them. It's serious business in her house. Trust me when I tell you that there wasn't a deadline to be missed. Keep in mind that this was back in the day before everyone had a laptop or Google drive. To be honest, even with a laptop and Google drive, I keep important documents in physical file folders. It makes me feel safe, so it works for me.

You and your child have to organize college application materials in a way that is easy for you and your student to keep track of them. This section will discuss keeping physical filing systems, using a calendar system to keep track of deadlines, creating a checklist for each school application, and downloading apps and wizards for the techies. Hold on tight.

Creating Physical Files

Filing isn't particularly difficult, unless you are me. The only way this filing thing works is if you consistently use a system. It doesn't matter how you label the files, or what you decide to put in the file. What matters is that you do the same thing each and every time with all the files. That is really the only way it works.

Start with some new manila file folders. On the tab, write the name of the college. When you open the folder, write the application, scholarship, financial aid, and deposit deadlines for the school on the top left side of the folder. On the right side of the manila folder, make note of the correspondence you have had with the school. For example, if your student sent the application, but the school sent a letter or e-mail stating that it is missing a recommendation letter, put the 'missing document' letter in the file, but note the date, the subject of the letter, and the resolution of the issue on the right side as a quick reference guide.

Colleges are usually kind enough to provide prospective students with some sort of application checklist. Many schools now allow applicants to check the status of all their materials online, so your student can easily look and make sure the admission department has all the necessary components. If the college also provides a physical checklist, that's awesome—and your student should use it. If not, you should create your own checklist for each file. The checklist should, at a minimum, list the following basic items:

- Transcript
- Recommendation letter(s)
- Application
- Essay(s)
- Financial aid
- Test scores

- Any additional items this college requires, such as a supplement, additional short essay responses, résumé, and so on

Make a note of when each of these items was sent or should be sent to the school. Remember that colleges may have multiple applications deadlines: you and your student will have to decide if he or she will apply early or regular decision, and then follow the appropriate deadlines for submitting materials. Depending on the college, early decision deadlines could be as early as October and regular decision deadlines as late as February. Keep in mind that the FAFSA for financial aid can't be filed until after January 1.

The Calendar Is King

Make your calendar your best friend during this process. I have the calendar connected to my e-mail, my cell phone calendar, a physical day planner, and a wall calendar. If something isn't on my calendar, you better believe it doesn't really exist to me. The college application deadlines are essential. You need to know when things are due at all times. For example, at some schools the scholarship deadline is different from the general financial aid deadline. If your student doesn't submit the scholarship application by the deadline, it won't matter about the valid financial need because he or she didn't apply on time. Deadlines are deadlines.

We don't want you missing any deadlines. So synchronize calendars with your child, your phone, your computer, and any other device you use to remind you of the important things in your life. Those reminders will be more important than ever in the coming application season. By thinking about these things near the end of your child's junior year, you can map out everything that needs to happen in advance and plan accordingly. Nothing should be sneaking up on you at the last minute next year.

Apps and Wizards

I am truly an analog girl. But for others, digital is the only way to go. There are so many tools available to help you stay organized and on track. If these kinds of digital tools are truly integrated into your life, here are some apps that may be effective for you and your student to use in the college application process.

Basic Calendar Creator (http://www.timeanddate.com/calendar/basic.html): This page allows you to create a basic customized calendar. This is one of the world's most popular websites regarding time and date.

Toodledo (http://www.toodledo.com/): If you don't want to use the checklists I outlined earlier, use Toodledo. It's a to-do list on steroids with a hotlist, customizable alarms, and a sortable online to-do list to help you remember to complete tasks on-time. It's available for your mobile phone, in your e-mail, on your calendar, integrated directly into your web browser, and more.

Asana (www.asana.com): If you love checklists as much as I do, you will love Asana—it's the best shared checklist ever. If you create a task in Asana, you can assign it to your student with a due date. Asana will remind you both via e-mail when the task's due date is coming or if it becomes past due.

College Application Wizard (http://collegeappwizard.com/): The College Application Wizard is a great tool that claims to be the most personalized, comprehensive, streamlined, and anxiety-reducing way to navigate college admission and financial aid applications. This tool does everything we have discussed with respect to checklists and organizing for you. It will remind you what to do and when to do it. To reduce future headaches, this may be worth checking out—and yes, it's free.

Checklists

If you don't feel like creating your own checklist from scratch for each college application file, or if the college didn't provide you with a checklist, here are some prepared ones that can take the guesswork out of the process.

My College Calendar (http://www.mycollegecalendar.org/explore/pdf/application-checklist-pdf.pdf)

College Board (https://bigfuture.collegeboard.org/get-in/applying-101/college-application-checklist): The College Board application checklist is pretty simple and easy to use. Check out the website listed, print out a copy, and stick it in each file folder for quick reference.

Campus Explorer (https://www.campusexplorer.com/registration/planner/?backref=%2Fmyplanner%2F): This site offers an interactive checklist. It also provides access to college searches, scholarships, financial aid tips, and more.

Prep Work for Parents, Too

While your student is busy finalizing their application materials, there's work you need to be doing, too—figuring out the finances so your child can go to college. It's wonderful to look at campuses and envision your student there, but who's going to pay for it and how? Are there schools that your child shouldn't even apply to because they're simply not financially feasible for your family?

Hopefully, this is something you've been thinking about and preparing for all along, since ninth grade when you and your child started discussing his or her interests and possible majors. The issue of college costs and skyrocketing student debt is a hot topic these days, and this is one life lesson you probably don't want your student to learn first-hand.

Because this is such an important subject, with so much material to cover, I've put the information in a separate chapter, **Chapter 6–Financial Fundamentals: Planning and Paying for College**. From saving for college to tips on filling out the FAFSA, you'll find it all there. The sooner you plan for the financial side of college, the better—don't wait until your student has an acceptance letter from their number-one choice to discover that you can't afford it.

Finally, It's Time to Apply

All the months of planning and preparation have come down to this—that moment when your student completes the application and hits "send." With most colleges handling their admission process online these days, it doesn't seem quite as momentous as putting all the forms, letters, and transcripts in an envelope and taking it to the post office in time to get a postmark before the deadline. But it's still a milestone moment. Here are some things to remember:

- While you and your student have no doubt looked at the college's admission requirements online numerous times since starting your search process, be sure to check one last time to make sure you are following all the guidelines and are submitting all the necessary items.

- Even if your student is applying to multiple schools using The Common Application, most schools have some additional requirements as well, such as a supplemental essay and questions specific to its institution. Don't forget those, or your student's application will be ignored.

- Since the admissions process is being handled online, you may not be able to be as involved as you want to be. Students are assigned a PIN number for the process, sometimes even before they can look at the application. Hopefully they will share that with you; if not, you and your student will have to trust them to take care of all the necessary steps and check online to make sure the college has received the other items it needs, such as test scores, class transcripts, and letters of recommendation.

- Most online forms allow students to work on their applications, then save them and come back to them again and again. That's good—there isn't the pressure of having to sit down and complete an application all at one time.

- Encourage your student not to wait until the last minute, but remember that these are teenagers who operate 24/7 in a last-minute mindset.

- Once your student has completed the application, ask if you can do a final review to make sure nothing has been forgotten before it is submitted. There is nothing worse than discovering you forgot to include something important 5 minutes after you sent the form.

- If your student is applying to multiple schools, there may be multiple application dates, sometimes months apart. Be sure to stay on top of all of them.

Once the applications have been submitted, then the waiting starts! Make note of when each school will notify applicants, and, until then, encourage your student to focus on other things—like keeping their senior-year grades strong. This is also a good time to shift gears and work on seeking out and applying for scholarships.

Acceptance or Rejection— Now What?

The applications and essays have been completed and sent. Then the waiting begins. Students who apply via early action or early decision may have a reply in a couple of weeks, sometimes as early as November or December. If your student applied regular decision to a big state school, it could be a couple of months, and the decision might not arrive until April. And while the waiting can be excruciating, receiving a response can be even harder. Is the envelope thick (good!) or thin (not so good)? Or, if the decision arrives via e-mail, your student is likely to hesitate before clicking on it, not knowing if the next few seconds will lead to elation or dejection.

This can be a joyous time, but it will also have its sad moments because your student may be rejected by one or more of the schools they applied to. Rejection is not fun. All of a sudden, the school that rejected your student will seem like a much better school than the one your child did get accepted to. I moped and cried when I got my rejection letter, but at the end of the day, it is a waste of valuable time. Now is the time to model gratefulness to your child.

And yes, you should be grateful, because your child is going to college. Your student will continue their education, lay the groundwork for a career, experience new things, make life-altering decisions, and hopefully mature into an adult. Who cares that some school sent a rejection letter? Savor the acceptance letters and celebrate your student's accomplishment. Your family is fortunate for this opportunity so it's time to move on from the safety, match, and reach piles. It's the acceptance pile that matters now.

Well, not just the acceptance letters—waitlist letters matter, too. When your student receives a waitlist letter it means that the school liked your student but didn't have enough room to accept him or her outright. Once the school receives responses from its accepted students and knows how many seats are available in its freshman class, the school may be able to send acceptance letters to waitlisted students. If your student contacts someone in the admission department and lets them know that he or she is still very interested in attending the school and asks to be put on the waitlist, there is a possibility that an acceptance letter could arrive at a later date. The tough part is the waiting—not knowing if that acceptance letter will ever show up, and then being prepared if it shows up very late, like in June. In the meantime, it's best to review the offers (and financial aid awards) from those schools that did offer admission to your student; it's the old "bird in the hand is worth two in the bush" scenario.

Check out **Chapter 6—Financial Fundamentals: Planning and Paying for College** for detailed information about financial aid award letters, types of financial aid—grants, private loans, federal loan programs, state-based aid, Federal Work-Study program, and scholarships.

Once you've compared the financial packages from the schools where your student was accepted, evaluated the financial aid options available to you, and applied for (and perhaps won!) some scholarships, it's time to move on to making the big decision.

Making That Last Big Choice

If your student gets an acceptance letter from that school they've had their heart set on throughout the entire process, the decision is easy. But what if your student has four acceptances and no clear-cut favorite? How do you narrow multiple acceptances to "the one"?

- Start with an old-fashioned pro/con list. Take a practical look at the options.

- Calculate how much each school is going to cost, and be realistic about what your family can afford. Compare each school's financial aid offer, and take a look at the financing options available.

- Have an honest conversation with your student and discuss the following:

  - What makes the most sense financially?

  - How much money can your family contribute to the process?

  - How much financial aid will your child be receiving?

  - Is the tuition manageable?

  - Will your child need to take out a student loan on their own, or will you need to co-sign?

  - Will your child need to apply for work study?

- Schedule one last visit to the schools, if necessary and time permits. Some schools do have specific days for accepted students and their parents to come and take one last look, observe classes, meet with administrators and professors, sample the food, and possibly stay overnight in the dorms with current students.

There is no such thing as the perfect college. It can be difficult when your student's favorite school is not a realistic option for your family. Your student's goal is a good fit and good investment in the long run. The college your student chooses is simply their environment for potential success and achievement—it's up to your child to make that happen!

Responding to Schools: Saying Yes and No

Once your student has made a decision, he or she needs to respond to each school that sent an offer. Sending a 'thank you, but no thank you' e-mail or letter to the admission department or counselor your child worked with is a basic courtesy and frees up space for other students who are eagerly awaiting this opportunity as well.

For the school your child plans to attend, they need to respond "Yes!" as soon as they have decided. Then you and your student will need to follow all the instructions the school provides, right down to the last detail. The school may supply an acceptance letter for you to fill out and return. Admission officials will always request that you respond with a deposit by a specific deadline. The deposit holds your student's spot, so send it in on time. The college may also request that you include a separate letter for financial aid. Whatever they tell you to do, do it. If you don't understand what you need to do next, call the admission or financial aid office at the school and ask questions. Whatever you do, don't miss the deadlines.

Be sure to check out the Summer Planning chapter that follows to get some ideas on how your child can spend his or her summer after graduation!

Well, that's it—four years of planning, preparation, and effort has resulted in your child achieving their goal of going to college. The time flew, didn't it? So take a moment to relax. Give thanks. You did your best to help your son or daughter!

While this is the end of one journey, it's just the beginning of the next one. In the next chapter, you will find every checklist imaginable, including one to help get your student off to college with everything he or she will most likely need. As you check everything off that list, make sure you grab some tissues for yourself.

SENIOR YEAR CHECKLIST

☐ If for some reason your child has not taken the ACT or SAT (or if the score isn't what your child had hoped), has he or she registered for a fall administration of the exam?

☐ When your child registered for the ACT or SAT, did he or she indicate target colleges to receive the scores?

☐ Have you taken stock of application requirements for your child's target schools?

　　– What documents must be compiled for a completed application?

　　– What are the deadlines?

　　– Have you created ticklers to remind you of due dates?

　　– Have you requested application fee waivers, if applicable?

☐ Have you contacted your student's counselor to make sure your child is on track for graduation?

☐ Have you determined whether your student needs to take any SAT Subject Tests?

☐ Have you filled out the FAFSA?

☐ Have you compared offers from schools at which your child was accepted?

☐ Have you compared the financial aid packages?

☐ Did your student inform the other schools that sent acceptance letters that he or she has chosen to attend another school?

☐ Did you send a commitment and deposit to your student's chosen school by the deadline?

☐ Did you accept the school's financial aid offer?

CHAPTER 5

The Path to College: List by List

When I was growing up, *CliffsNotes*™ was a popular study tool that allowed students to skip some parts of our dense reading assignments (even though we really were not supposed to do that!). *CliffsNotes* provided summaries of various books—covering the essential points—and allowed students to learn much of what they needed about a book without necessarily reading all of it.

So think of this section as a *CliffsNotes* for college preparation. You may not have time to read every word of every chapter, or maybe you discovered this book a little later in your student's educational journey. This chapter can help you get to the nitty-gritty on *getting ahead of the curve* and let you see what you can apply immediately to get the job done.

If you've skimmed through this book, you've seen that each chapter has its own checklist of things parents should do at various stages of their student's high school career, and I've included these lists in this chapter, too. I've included such important items as a test-preparation checklist, questions to ask college admissions officers, and a handy form for tracking every step of the college application process. If you find something here that you'd like to know more about, you can quickly refer to the appropriate chapter for that information. Even if you've read each chapter line by line, I hope this section will be a great quick reference for you.

Checklist of Questions to Ask Your Student's Guidance Counselor

1) What percentage of your school's students graduate from high school?

2) What percentage of your school's students attends college after graduation?

3) What are the average PSAT/NMSQT, ACT, and SAT scores at the school?

4) On average, are there any test problem subjects for students at the school?

5) Does the school offer the ACT Plan and Explore in addition to the PSAT/NMSQT to students in grades 9 and 10?

6) Can the counselor provide you with a copy of your child's proposed ninth-grade course schedule?

7) Does the school offer academic support programs for struggling students and in what subjects?

8) Does the school offer general, vocational or tech-prep, and college-prep diplomas?

9) Can the counselor provide you with a copy of your school's graduation requirements for a college-prep diploma?

10) Can the counselor provide you with a copy of a sample college-prep academic course schedule?

11) Does the school offer Advanced Placement (AP) or International Baccalaureate (I.B.) courses?

12) What courses would the counselor recommend for a college-bound student?

13) What are the prerequisite courses for the more challenging courses on the college-prep schedule, and is there a minimum GPA requirement for those courses?

14) Does the counselor recommend any local summer programming for a college-bound student?

Academic Schedule Checklist

To create a college-prep curriculum, gather the following:

- Any standardized test results you have available
- Your student's report cards for the past two years

- Any important notes from teachers regarding your child's progress or academic standing for the past two years
- The proposed course schedule for the current academic year (if you can get all four years, even better)
- A list of all academic support options available at the school
- A list of all electives available at the school and course descriptions, if available
- Notes on your personal observations of your student's strengths and weaknesses
- Input from your child on his or her academic standing and where improvement may be needed

To help map out the right college-prep courses, here are some key steps:

Step 1: Break down your student's schedule by semester or quarter, depending on how the school's academic schedule is structured.

Step 2: Print a blank calendar and write in each core class your student will take for the year.

Step 3: Select electives based on areas where your student needs help. For example, if your son is not a strong writer, one elective course you may want him to consider is creative writing. Another potential option would be a logical reasoning/critical thinking–based course to help him with idea development.

Step 4: Scout out any study hall periods or other downtime available in the schedule. If academic support is available at your school, schedule it during a study hall. See if a school-based tutor or an outside tutor can work with your student during that time. At the end of each grading period, review your student's progress, and determine whether any adjustments need to be made. Keep any new test results, teacher comments, and grade reports in the above-mentioned file.

Checklist to Stay on Track in Tenth Grade

Even though graduation may seem far in the future, tenth grade is an important time to be thinking ahead, planning, and laying the academic groundwork your child will need to go to college. Here's a quick checklist of things you and your child should keep working on this year:

- Set up an appointment with your child's guidance counselor to verify that your child is on track with the right courses for the year ahead.

- Does your child have a list of five potential choices for a college major?

- If not, ask your child to list the top five activities he or she really likes and create a list of possible majors. Encourage your child to research potential careers associated with each major or activity.

- Encourage your student to set up an appointment with his or her guidance counselor—a meeting *you* won't attend. Help your child prepare for this meeting by writing down questions to ask regarding his or her interests and recommendations the counselor can make about future courses and meaningful activities.

- Talk with your student about the importance of maintaining consistent grades throughout the year.

- Discuss the effectiveness of study groups or even a study buddy, and determine if this method would be beneficial for your son or daughter.

- Has your child made good choices in terms of extracurricular activities at school or in the community? Has your student committed to sticking with the activity for at least one year?

- Do those activities fit with your student's academic schedule—as well as your family's schedule? Is your student able to maintain his or her grades while participating in extracurricular activities?

- Did your child take a practice PSAT/NMSQT exam?
- Have you and your student determined a meaningful way to spend the summer after tenth grade, such as an enrichment program, a summer job, volunteer work, and so on?

Test-Prep Checklist

- Set specific day(s) and time(s) for your child to prepare for the test each week. It doesn't necessarily have to be the same time each week, but it's important to make regular practice a scheduled priority.
- Find a timer for your child to use when practicing under time constraints. There are free online applications that can be used to do this, too.
- Make sure your child's study space is conducive to studying—large enough to spread out the material and with few distractions. If need be, agree that you should take possession of your child's phone during study time to minimize potential interruptions.
- Make sure the study space is stocked with supplies like pencils, highlighters, and note cards.
- Have a signal, note, or some sign that your child can use to let the rest of the family know he or she is studying and should not be disturbed during those test-prep times.
- Buy some earplugs that your child can use to filter out household activity, just in case.
- Have some healthy refreshments in the room for your child to have easy access to on prep days.
- Make sure your child has registered for the SAT and/or ACT and that he or she has the admission ticket in a safe place (print this out after registering online).
- Work backwards from the test date to create your child's test-prep schedule.

- Go online to the ACT and SAT websites to find which calculator (if any) is acceptable for your child to use on the exam. If your student doesn't already have an acceptable one, purchase one so he or she can practice with it before test day.

- Have your student take a diagnostic practice test that will provide a baseline score so you can best assess his or her strengths and weaknesses.

- If necessary, find a tutor, community program, or test-prep service to help your student prepare for the exam.

Questions to Answer before Senior Year

Fall:

- Has your student created an e-mail account specifically for college correspondence yet? If not, he or she should. Make sure the address created is simple and professional—not *GamerDude4ever* or *luvs2shop.*

- Did your child take the PSAT/NMSQT in October?

- Did you receive the PSAT/NMSQT score report?

- If your child qualified to advance in the NMSQT competition, did he or she submit the additional information requested?

- Did you review the PSAT score report for strengths and weaknesses in particular subjects?

- Did you and your child plan and decide when he or she will take the SAT and/or ACT? Has your student registered for those tests?

Winter:

- Did you and your child begin narrowing down the list of colleges?

- Do any of the schools on that target list prefer one college entrance exam over the other?

- Does your student have a preference? ACT or SAT?
- Will your child be taking a test-prep course? Has he or she registered for that course?
- If not, did you purchase a test-prep book and create a schedule based on the timeline in the book?
- Did you sign up for any of the free test-prep resources?
- Did your child take the December SAT?
- Did you receive the SAT results with the detailed study plan?
- Did your child take a practice ACT over winter break?
- Did your student sit for the February ACT?

Spring:

- Have you and your student evaluated and sorted the colleges on their list?
- Have you scheduled college visits at your student's safe, match, and reach schools?
- Have you started on the list of potential recommenders? Did all the teachers on that list teach your child within the previous two academic years?
- Did you pull all the essay prompts and questions from the application and/or websites from the colleges on your student's target list?
- Have you and your student created a calendar for all the upcoming deadlines? Remember to include other important dates on that calendar as well, such as midterms, AP exams, and finals, so you can plan accordingly.
- Did you create a file folder for each of the schools on your final list and a checklist for each school?

Summer:

- Have you spoken with the potential recommenders about whether they would write a letter for your student?

- Did you and your student visit the colleges on the list?
- Does your student have all the applications for each college?
- Do you have all the necessary deadlines outlined on your calendar and your child's calendar?
- Has your student completed one or two college essays and submitted them to a teacher or mentor for review?
- Are you ready for your student's senior year?

Recommendation Letters Checklist

Good letters of recommendation don't just happen—they're part of a process. Here are some steps for your student to follow:

- Select your recommenders.
- Create a separate file for each recommender.
- Avoid making requests around midterms, final exams, the first week of class, and holidays and vacations.
- Include a statement of goals/aspirations.
- Give context for the letter to the recommender.
- Provide an addressed and stamped envelope (or details on how and where the letter can be submitted online).
- Provide contact information in case the recommender has any questions.
- Provide talking points for the letter.
- Give some background, if necessary
- Follow up by your in-house deadline to ensure the letter was sent.
- Send a thank-you note to each recommender.

Application Checklist

TO DO:	College 1	College 2	College 3	College 4
Download application				
Submit for early decision/date				
Submit for regular decision/date				
Send ACT scores				
Send SAT scores				
Send SAT Subject Test scores				
Send AP Test scores				
Recommendation letters requested:				
1._____				
2._____				
3._____				
Recommendation letters sent to schools				
Thank you notes sent				
Essays drafted				
Essays reviewed by 2 people				
Essays completed				
Transcript requested (fall)				
Transcript requested (spring)				
Complete FAFSA				
Submit CSS/Financial Aid Profile				
Complete school aid form (if applicable)				
Complete state aid form (if applicable)				
Apply for scholarships				
Acceptance letter received				
Financial aid award letter received				
Commitment letter sent				
Deposit sent				

FAFSA Documents Checklist

- Your student's Social Security number
- Your student's Alien Registration number (if not a U.S. citizen)
- Your most recent federal income tax returns, W-2s, and other records of money earned
- Your bank statements and records of investments (if applicable)
- Your records of untaxed income (if applicable)
- A Federal Student Aid PIN to sign electronically, which you get by going to www.pin.ed.gov

Financial Aid Checklist

- Is my child eligible for a Pell Grant?
- Are campus-based grants available?
- Are there career-based grant programs based on my child's proposed major?
- What private loans are a fit for my family?
- Is my child eligible for the Direct Subsidized Loan Program? How much?
- Is my child eligible for the Direct Unsubsidized Loan Program? How much?
- Is my child eligible for a Perkins Loan? How much?
- Is my child eligible for the Direct PLUS Loan program? How much?
- Is my child eligible for state-based aid? How much?
- Is my child eligible for Federal Work-Study?
- Is my child eligible for any scholarships? Which ones? Has he or she completed the necessary applications and essays? When are the applications due?
- How much savings do we have to assist with tuition?

Senior Year Checklist

August/September

- Register for the ACT/SAT, if necessary—meaning if your child for some reason has yet to take the test or if the score isn't what he or she hoped it would be.
- Take stock of application requirements.
  - What documents must be compiled for a completed application?
  - What are the deadlines?
  - Create ticklers to remind you of due dates.
- See your student's counselor and make sure your child is on track for graduation.
- Determine whether or not AP exams and SAT Subject Tests must be taken.

October/November

- Early deadlines will begin around this time so have your completed application by this time.
- Request fee waivers, if applicable.
- Request transcripts.
- Verify your ACT/SAT test scores were sent.
- FAFSA will be released. You cannot submit until January 1, but you need to become familiar with the application and the documents you need.

December

- Regular decisions will be due January/February, so have your applications organized prior to the deadline.

January/February

- Complete the FAFSA application ASAP after January 1.
- Verify that your first semester transcripts were sent.
- Take the last accepted administration of the ACT/SAT for your college application cycle.

March/April

- At this point, your child will begin receiving responses from colleges.
- Compare financial aid packages.
- Make final visits to colleges that your child has been accepted to, if necessary.
- Make that final college decision.

May

- Send a commitment and deposit by the deadline.
- Follow all financial aid instructions.
- Request the final transcript.

Packing for College Checklist

Helping a student pack for college may not be as challenging as getting them through the past four years, but it's still a big and potentially costly task. Of course, each student's situation will vary. The student who goes to a college nearby and comes home for a visit once a month won't need to take as much as the student who is packing for the entire year to attend a school hundreds of miles away, or in a different climate. And a student who is going to live in an apartment will probably need a lot more to set up housekeeping than a dorm dweller.

If your student is one of those who is going far away, you may want to consider purchasing some items via national retailers (such as Bed, Bath, and Beyond) that can ship items directly to your student's dorm, or hold them at the retailer's location in the city nearest your student's college. Or students can wait and shop for the items they need when they get to campus.

Before packing anything, check the college's website for a list of items that may be recommended or forbidden. Different schools have different policies regarding appliances, furnishings, and even computers; it makes no sense to buy a microwave if it's not allowed in your student's dorm room.

Here are some tried and true things to remember:

Clothing:

- Comfortable and appropriate clothes and shoes (unless they've worn a uniform, the clothes they wore for high school will probably be fine)
- Outdoor/seasonal wear (raincoat, umbrella, boots, gloves, mittens, scarves, and hats and a winter coat for cold-weather climates)
- Sportswear (appropriate gear and clothing for whatever your student might be participating in at school, whether it's soccer or yoga)
- Bathrobe, loungewear, pajamas
- Underwear, socks
- Dressy clothes (for that awards banquet, job interview, or formal)

Personal Care Items:

Do you need to send enough for the entire year or will they buy their own as needed—or help themselves to yours when they come home for weekends and breaks?

- Shower shoes
- Shampoo/conditioner/other hair-care products
- Comb and brush
- Razors/shave cream
- Toothbrush, toothpaste, and dental floss
- Deodorant
- Makeup
- Feminine hygiene items
- Plastic tote for carrying supplies back and forth to the bathroom
- Lip balm
- First aid kit
- Headache/pain/fever medicine
- Cold/allergy medicine
- Cough drops
- Tissues: a box for their room and packets for their backpack
- Toilet paper (depends on the school)
- Any other medications your student may use on a regular basis

Linens:

Be sure to check with the college before buying sheets for dormitory beds; most of those require twin extra-long sheets.

- Towels and washcloths
- Sheets
- Pillows
- Blankets
- Comforter
- Fleece throw

Appliances and Electronics:

Again, check to see if these items are allowed in student housing. If students can't have a refrigerator and/or microwave in their room, they are usually provided for student use in the residence hall.

- Microwave
- Mini-fridge
- Iron
- Blow-dryer and other hair-care/personal-care devices
- Power strip (for all those chargers and electronic devices)
- Computer (probably a laptop; consider getting a removable hard drive and encouraging your student to back up their system regularly, just in case their computer is damaged or stolen)
- Flash drive—perhaps more than one
- Printer—Check first because many schools have printers available in the residence halls and throughout the campus for student use, and many assignments are submitted electronically, not on paper.
- Cell phone
- Gaming systems and hand-held video games
- TV—Keep in mind though that most residence halls have shared TVs, and students today do most of their viewing online with their laptop or other devices.
- Simple tool kit
- Sticky-tack for hanging posters and photos on the walls (again, check the school policy about what is acceptable)

Desk/School Supplies:

- Notebooks and paper
- Pens, pencils, erasers
- Scissors, tape

- Backpack/book bag/laptop case
- Address book with family contact information
- Stamps and letter-writing supplies (yes, if prodded, they might send Grandma a note!)

Snacks, Treats, and Miscellaneous:

- Microwave popcorn
- Instant hot chocolate, tea, or coffee drink packets
- Gum and mints
- Favorite snacks, sealed in individual packets (granola bars, chips, crackers, cookies, and so on)
- Shelf-stable meal items that can be prepared with a microwave or hot water (ramen noodles, single-servings of mac and cheese, instant oatmeal, canned soup, and so on)
- Paper plates and plastic eating utensils
- Gift cards (Target, Barnes and Noble, Walgreens, Pizza Hut, Starbucks, and so on)
- Board or card games (great for making new friends)
- Home-away-from-home items (photo albums, stuffed animals, and so on)
- Sports equipment
- Musical instrument
- Favorite books, DVDs

Cleaning Supplies:

These may be optional, depending on the school your student chooses to attend and their own standards for a clean living area!

- Laundry detergent and fabric softener (the self-contained detergent pods are great for college students as are dryer sheets)

- Quarters for laundry (although most schools use a swipe-card system now)
- Hamper, laundry bag, or laundry basket
- Cleaning wipes
- Disinfectant wipes
- Air freshener
- Bathroom cleaner
- Mop, broom, or a dry floor duster
- Paper towels

Things Your Student Needs to Know/Have Access to:

- Their Social Security number (stress the importance of keeping it secure)
- Your family's health insurance information (or card if your child has one)
- Personal financial materials (debit or ATM card, checkbook, online access to accounts)
- Contact information for their personal/family physician
- Insurance information for their personal belongings

CHAPTER 6

Financial Fundamentals: Planning and Paying for College

COLLEGE BOUND

There are numerous ways to save money for college. While I am not an expert in college savings, I can give you a couple of options that are popular and workable, with some planning and commitment. Keep in mind that the earlier you start saving for college, the more your student will benefit. While saving since your child was born would be ideal, it's not realistic for most of us. But even four years of savings effort can produce results.

Saving for College

There are four options that I will discuss in this section: SAGE Scholars Tuition Rewards Program, the 529 savings plan, Upromise, and mutual funds.

SAGE Scholars Tuition Rewards® Program

The SAGE Scholars Tuition Rewards® Program (TRP) is a privately administered college savings program that rewards investment dollars with scholarship "points" that can be used at more than 320 colleges nationwide. It's like earning frequent flyer miles or other cash-back rewards. Here's how it works.

When you make deposits into a qualifying account at one or more of the TRP participating financial institutions you earn annual points based on the value of your investment. The points aren't redeemed for money but are converted into discounts on college tuition. Participating colleges are contractually bound to give participants a reduction in tuition costs; each point equals $1 in tuition.

The fact that the points aren't hard dollars in your account is an important distinction. Because the points you accumulate through the program aren't considered assets, your Expected Family Contribution doesn't take a hit when the Department of Education calculates financial aid for your child.

The national list of participating schools is available at www. tuitionrewards.com. If any of your child's target schools are on this list, you may want to consider this program. You do have to enroll before your student enters eleventh grade.

Finally, be mindful that the national list for SAGE is limited. So, if you don't see any of your child's target schools on the list, don't fret. One of the other options listed in this section could be a better fit.

529 Savings Plans

In 1996, the IRS created the 529 plan to help families save money for future college expenses. The government offers tax advantages for those who invest in the plan. While the plan's name comes from Section 529 in the Federal Internal Revenue Code, the program is administered by individual states and agencies. Each state determines its plan's structure and what type of investment options to offer. Individual states may also offer their own tax benefits associated with these plans.

There are two types of 529 plans: prepaid and savings.

The prepaid plan lets participants buy tuition credits at today's rates and then use those credits in the future when their children are in college. By prepaying, you are protecting yourself from tuition inflation. Only a dozen or so states have a prepaid plan.

The 529 savings plan helps you generate money for college based on the earnings of the underlying investment, which are usually mutual funds. Virtually all states offer this type of 529 savings plan.

According to the College Savings Plans Network, there are many benefits to 529 plans, such as the following:

- The earnings are exempt from state and federal income tax; some states also allow tax exemptions for contributions.

- Withdrawals from the plan used specifically for qualified higher education expenses are exempt from federal income tax.
- Depending on the state, withdrawals for qualified higher education expenses may also be exempt from state income tax.
- The minimum contribution can be as low as $15 per month.
- The beneficiary can be changed at any time to another member of the beneficiary's family.
- The funds can be used at almost any school in the United States.
- Your 529 funds can pay for tuition, fees, room, board, books, supplies, and required equipment.
- Assets within 529 plans are protected from bankruptcy.

The 529 program is a great resource that is used by millions of parents each year. Plan details for each state are available online. SavingForCollege.com is a good place to start investigating what options are available to you. Check out www.savingforcollege. com/529_plan_details/.

Upromise®

Upromise® is a corporation owned by Sallie Mae (the Student Loan Marketing Association) that helps you earn as you spend, much like a credit card rewards program. To participate, you create a Upromise account, then with every purchase at participating grocery or drug stores, restaurants, local retailers, or online stores, you can earn money that can later be used toward college tuition.

The Upromise network includes over 20,000 grocery and drug stores, more than 10,000 restaurants, and over 850 online stores. When you eat at a participating restaurant, you earn 8 percent back, and when you shop online, you receive 5 percent back. Electronic coupons available on the website earn you money when you use them at participating grocery and drug stores.

You can learn more and register for the program at www.upromise.com.

Mutual Funds

Direct investing is when an investor purchases his or her own stock. An example of a direct investment would be purchasing your own stocks on E*Trade. Alternatively, a mutual fund would be considered an 'indirect' investment. When you invest in a mutual fund, your money goes into a 'pool' with money from other investors. Collectively, that money is used by the mutual fund to purchase securities. By investing in the fund, you are purchasing shares in the fund as a stockholder. As the mutual fund makes money on the investments made, the stockholders share in its profits. With many mutual funds, you are even able to buy and sell your shares of the fund at any time. They are said to be great for long-term investments and are often used for retirement or education planning.

I'll be the first to admit that mutual funds are outside my area of expertise. They may be outside yours as well. However, given the long and seemingly credible history of mutual funds and recent news that many funds have been outpacing inflating college costs, you may want to do some research to determine if this investment is right for you. There are many mutual funds to choose from—so many that choosing one could be a daunting task. I recommend that you speak with a financial advisor to see which fund can best meet your needs.

The idea of paying for college is enough to cause anyone to panic. But panic is not the proper response. You need to stay clear-headed and realistic. With proper planning, contributing toward your child's college tuition is possible, and doing so can help reduce the amount of your student's future debt. Here are some important points to remember about college savings:

- There are many more savings options than those listed in this chapter. Start with the ones I've mentioned but do some additional research to find what best fits your family.

- How can you learn more about saving for college? Talk to people you trust on money matters: your banker or financial adviser. Your student's guidance counselor can refer you to any public seminars or informational meetings on this topic. You can also find a lot of information online.

- Thoroughly investigate any financial program before you commit to it.

- When it comes to college savings, the earlier you start the better. If you haven't done anything to this point, get started now.

Starting the Financial Aid Process

All college financial aid begins with the Free Application for Student Aid, also known as FAFSA (https://fafsa.ed.gov/).

Applying For Aid: What is the FAFSA?

Though every college-bound student needs to file the FAFSA, not everyone understands how it works. To learn everything you need to know about this form and process, download the comprehensive guide at http://studentaid.ed.gov/sites/default/files/2014-15-completing-fafsa.pdf.

This guide has all you need to know about applying for financial aid to help pay your student's college expenses. Many schools or school districts also host programs about the college financial aid process, or provide assistance in filling out and filing the FAFSA. Check with your student's school or guidance counselor to see if any of these programs are coming up in your area. It's always good to have access to a real person to answer your questions or lend a hand.

Here are some additional tips to ensure your FAFSA application process is less stressful and more successful.

Make a FAFSA file that includes everything you'll need to apply. You will need the following documents to accurately and completely fill out the FAFSA and other financial aid application forms:

- Your student's Social Security number

- Your student's Alien Registration number (if not a U.S. citizen)

- Your most recent federal income tax returns, W-2s, and other records of money earned

- Your bank statements and records of investments (if applicable)

- Your records of untaxed income (if applicable)

- A Federal Student Aid PIN to sign electronically, which you get by going to www.pin.ed.gov

Individual schools to which you apply may also ask for a copy of your W-2s to verify the information you submitted to FAFSA, so don't be surprised if you are asked to submit them. Having the documents ready when you apply makes it easier to go through the application process.

Don't wait! Don't be late! January 1 is the first day you can file the FAFSA, and it's important to file as early as possible since financial aid dollars are limited.

There is a "FAFSA on the Web Worksheet," which provides a preview of the questions that you will be asked on the actual form. You can find the worksheet here: http://studentaid.ed.gov/sites/default/files/2014-15-fafsa-worksheet.pdf. The information in purple is to be filled out by parents. It is a four-page worksheet and not terribly difficult. You may need to help your student fill out their section, especially if taxes have been filed in your child's name previously. You don't have to do this until your student's senior year, but it's good to know it's available online so you can see what it looks like and what you need to have so you can plan accordingly.

Your taxes are essential to your student's financial aid. The government bases the aid your student is eligible for on your total household income. Any delay in filing your income taxes will cause a delay in your student's financial aid, so if you often procrastinate until the April 15 deadline, this is **not** the year to do that! Your goal is to file your income taxes as soon as you have all the necessary information and are able to do so. Delays can cause your student to miss out on much-needed financial aid. However, you may not have all the necessary paperwork right away—employers have until

January 31 to provide W-2s, and other paperwork can arrive even in February. While it's easier to file the FAFSA after you've done your annual income taxes, if your household's financial situation is the same as it has been in recent years, you can fill in the form right away using the previous year's information so long as you indicate that you have done so. Then, update the FAFSA after you have filed your federal tax return and have all the current numbers.

Your student can list up to ten schools (each has a unique code number, usually available on its website) on the FAFSA worksheet. Once the school number is entered, FAFSA will send your student's award letter, also known as your Student Aid Report, to the schools indicated. Then, if your child is accepted at any of the schools you listed on the FAFSA application, the school will already have your financial information and can prepare a financial aid package.

Keep in mind that there are different federal, state, and school deadlines for filing financial aid information. You may want to create a spreadsheet to keep track of financial aid deadlines if you are juggling states and schools with different deadlines. You can check deadline dates here: http://www.fafsa.ed.gov/deadlines.htm.

Each school to which your student applies will have its own application and/or financial aid deadlines. Sometimes the college application and financial aid deadlines are the same, and sometimes they are not. FAFSA can be filed anytime between January 1 and June 30, but it's better not to wait. The sooner you do, the sooner your Student Aid Report can be prepared and sent to the school, hopefully well before its deadline.

Furthermore, many financial aid awards, specifically need-based and work-study programs, are often allocated on a first-come, first-served basis. The sooner your Student Aid Report gets to the school, the better chance your student will receive the funds they qualify for.

Transfer your FAFSA data automatically. The IRS has a nifty little tool that allows you to transfer your tax information directly to the FAFSA form. It's called the IRS Data Retrieval Tool, and it can be found at: https://fafsa.ed.gov/help/irshlp9.htm.

To use the tool just follow these simple steps:

- Enter your student's PIN (that you created when you began the FAFSA process) and click the hyperlink titled "Link to IRS."

- Your FAFSA will be saved, and you will be transferred to the IRS website.

- On the IRS website, enter the requested information.

- Once the IRS has validated your identification, your IRS tax information will display. You can either transfer your information from the IRS, or choose to return to "FAFSA on the Web," from the IRS website.

- If you do not transfer your information or choose not to return from the IRS website, you will have to log in to open your saved FAFSA.

- If you transfer your IRS tax information, questions on the FAFSA form that require tax information will be marked with "Transferred from the IRS."

This simple process ensures that many of the important numbers are transferred consistently and accurately from your tax forms to the FAFSA. There's still some more you need to do to complete the FAFSA application, but this tool makes it easier. And you will use it again and again, because yes, you have to file the FAFSA each year your student is in college!

What is the CSS/Financial Aid PROFILE®?

In addition to the FAFSA, some schools (usually private colleges) require the CSS/Financial Aid PROFILE® (PROFILE) through the College Board. The PROFILE is an online application that collects information used by certain colleges and scholarship programs to award financial aid.

Check with each of the schools your student is interested in, and see if they require it. If so, you can find the PROFILE at http://student. collegeboard.org/css-financial-aid-profile. It's designed to give member institutions a closer look at the finances of the applicant and his or her family. It is much more detailed than the FAFSA application and costs $25 dollars per college to file. However, fee waivers are available.

You will need to gather the following information before filling out the CSS PROFILE application:

- Current year federal income tax return(s), if completed
- Previous year federal income tax return(s)
- W-2 forms and other records of money earned in current year
- Records of untaxed income and benefits for previous and current year
- Current bank statements
- Current mortgage information
- Records of savings, stocks, bonds, trusts, and other investments
- E-mail address of a noncustodial parent, if applicable

You can find the complete instructions here: https://profileonline. collegeboard.org/prf/VignetteServlet/VignetteServlet. srv?relativePath=/profile/pdfs/1415_profile_instructions_drupal.pdf.

Financial Aid Award Letters

After your child receives an acceptance letter from a college or university, the next thing to come in the mail is the financial aid award letter. The award letter will detail the type of financial aid being offered to your child based on your FAFSA submission (and CSS PROFILE, if that was required also). The award letter can be a little confusing so I will try to break it down as much as possible.

There are four things you should focus on when looking at your award letter:

1) **Total Cost of Attendance:** This includes tuition, room and board, meal plans, fees, and other essential costs.

2) **Estimated Financial Contribution (EFC):** This is the amount of money (out of pocket) that the government estimates that your family will contribute to your child's education expenses.

3) **Your Financial Need:** This is the amount of money left over once you subtract your EFC from the cost of attendance. (This amount is what you hope scholarships and grants will cover so that you or your student won't have to take out loans to fill in the gap.)

4) **Financial Aid Award:** This is the amount of money awarded to your child in grants, scholarships, and/or federal and state aid. Be sure to look at the details of this very carefully; often schools will include a "standard" $5,000 loan as part of this, based on the assumption that these days, everyone will need to take out at least one loan. Remember, if it's a loan, your student or you will have to pay it back—it's not really an "award."

To help make this a little clearer, let's take a look at the following example:

	College A	College B	College C
Cost of Attendance	$41,000	$15,000	$22,000
Estimated Financial Contribution (EFC)	$7,000	$7,000	$7,000
Your Financial Need	$34,000	$8,000	$15,000
Financial Aid Award	$31,750	$6,400	$14,000
Unmet Need	$2,250	$1,600	$1,000
Your Total Costs (EFC plus Unmet Need)	$9,250	$8,600	$8,000

With **College A,** the cost of attendance is high. However, the school seems to be offering a large amount of financial aid (Financial Aid Award). When looking at the chart, it is important to keep in mind that EFC is an out-of-pocket cost. So unless you plan on obtaining a private loan for the EFC amount, it will be an out-of-pocket expense that will have to be paid directly to the college. In addition to the EFC amount, you will have to cover the unmet need amount as well. For College A, the total cost that would have to be covered is $9,250. This number may sound high, but let's see how it compares to the other schools.

Although the cost of attendance at Colleges B and C are significantly lower than College A, you can see that the out-of-pocket costs are not. College B's out-of-pocket costs would be $8,600. For College C, the out-of-pocket costs would be $8,000. College B is offering the smallest award amount, and College A is offering the largest award amount. Yet, the out-of-pocket costs aren't significantly different. If these are your student's top three schools, you and your child will need to determine whether to attend the school that offers a good amount of aid or the one with the lower tuition. This decision may be influenced by factors other than financial aid, since in this case, the cost to the family is about the same. What are the travel costs for each school? What is the cost of living once the student isn't in a residence hall or on a meal plan? Will the aid be available for the following academic years? Was one school a better fit than another? Does the school offer just a single major that your student is interested in—or are there plenty of Plan B options available should your child change his or her major?

Grab your calculator and figure out exactly what each school is offering your child and how much of the need is unmet. This will help you figure out which offer to accept and which to reject. Sometimes, if a school really wants your child to attend, it may match an offer given by another school, but you usually have to ask and the school may ask to see the offer from the competing school. Also, as other students commit to a school, it can free up some additional funds at the schools they reject. So as the May 1 deadline for committing to a college approaches, schools may be able to offer a little more financial assistance to students they would like to have attend who haven't yet made a decision, in hopes that sweetening the deal a little might get them to commit.

Types of Aid

In addition to the amount, the financial aid letter will tell you the type of aid your child will receive. Aid can come in several forms: grants, private or federal loans, state aid, federal work-study, and/or scholarships.

Grants

A grant is need-based aid that does not have to be repaid. Here are the various types of grants:

Pell Grants: A Pell Grant is generally considered to be the foundation of a student's financial aid package, to which other forms of aid are added. Each academic year, the U.S. Department of Education's Office of Financial Aid sets a maximum amount of Pell Grant aid a student may receive. For 2014–15, the maximum is $5,785. This amount, however, is not guaranteed. The amount a student receives depends on the amount the student needs, the cost of the school, whether the student is full- or part-time, and if the student plans to attend school for the full academic year.

Campus-based grants: There is another federal grant program called the Federal Supplemental Education Opportunity Grant (FSEOG). The maximum for this grant is $4,000. The difference between this grant and the Pell Grant is:

- This grant is given by the school based on funds allocated by the U.S. Department of Education to the school.
- Once the funds run out, no other students can receive the grant, whereas the Pell Grant is available to every student who meets the criteria.

In addition, if your child plans to attend an in-state school, there may be state-based grants available through the individual campus.

Career-based grants: These grants are given to students who commit to a certain major and set of classes and then take a particular job after graduation. In addition, students are required to stay within that field of study for a certain number of years in order to prevent the grant from converting into a loan. For example, the Teacher Education Assistance for College and Higher Education (TEACH) Grant Program offers up to $4,000 a year to students who are completing or plan to complete course work needed to begin a teaching career. To receive this grant, a student must agree to become a teacher in a high-need field at a school in a low-income area for at least four academic years, among other requirements.

Private Loans

This is aid that has to be repaid but is not based on need. Generally speaking, private loans are not need-based, and they are not going to be subsidized by the government in any way. Private loans are the kinds of loans your child can apply for to fund the shortfalls we discussed earlier (such as having enough savings to cover the freshman year but not the additional years). They often require parents to commit to cosigning the loan for their child and repaying the loan if the student fails to pay. The interest rate is generally determined based on credit, but it can also be based on other criteria. You can obtain these private loans through banks, private organizations, and/or foundations, and colleges often offer loans to their students. Check with the financial aid office at your student's proposed school to find out what options the representatives recommend.

Federal Loan Programs

There are four loan programs offered by the federal government.

Direct Subsidized Loan Program (Stafford): This program allows students with financial need to obtain a loan for their undergraduate education. The loan amount is determined by the school and cannot exceed the student's financial need, which means that your student won't be getting any additional funds once financial aid is processed. The perk to this loan program is that the U.S. Department of Education pays the interest on the loan while your student is in school at least part time, during a six-month grace period after graduation, and during deferment.

Direct Unsubsidized Loan Program (Stafford): This program is not based on need and is available to both undergraduate and graduate students. Like the subsidized program, the school determines the amount the student can receive by factoring in the other loans the student may have in addition to the one being applied for.

Perkins Loan Program: This is a school-based program that provides low-interest loans to students who demonstrate extreme financial need. The maximum available each year depends on individual need, the amount of other aid the student receives, and the availability of funds at the school.

Direct PLUS Loan Program: This program is credit based; the borrower must not have an adverse credit history. The parent of a dependent undergraduate student applies on behalf of the child enrolled at least part time in school. The maximum amount is the cost of attendance at the school minus all other financial aid received.

State-Based Aid

Most states offer some sort of aid to students who are residents of their state and plan to attend college in their state. The U.S. Department of Education website has a State Education Agency Directory (http://wdcrobcolp01.ed.gov/Programs/EROD/org_list. cfm?category_ID=SHE), which has the contact information for the appropriate agency in your state. By contacting this agency, you should be able to determine the state eligibility requirements and whether your child must attend school in your home state to obtain aid. But even if your child plans to attend school out of state, it doesn't hurt to check with that school's state agency to see if there are any aid programs available for out-of-state students; sometimes states have special programs giving students in neighboring states a break on tuition.

Federal Work-Study

Federal Work-Study is a federally based program that funds part-time employment for students based on financial need. Students can be employed by the school itself or by another designated agency. The funds that would normally be paid to the student are applied directly to the student's tuition. Students must fill out the FAFSA form in order to be eligible to apply for the Federal Work-Study program.

Scholarships

There are thousands of scholarships available to college students. Scholarships are offered by colleges and universities, businesses, community organizations, professional groups, individuals, religious organizations, and more. It just takes some effort to find them and determine if your student qualifies for them.

Here are some things to remember if you and your student are hoping to supplement your college funds via scholarships:

- While scholarships can certainly pay off, they're not a sure thing. Don't commit to a college that may be out of reach for you financially on the assumption that your student will win enough scholarships to pay for it. To be safe you still need to plan to cover your EFC and any additional unmet need without scholarships—then if your child does win some, it's a bonus.

- Completing the applications early, following instructions to the letter, and being organized are important; scholarship applications submitted at the last-minute are often lacking.

- Don't just focus on the amount; while a five-digit scholarship is certainly attractive, even a $1,000 award can cover the cost of books for a few semesters and make a difference. How long would your child have to work at a minimum-wage part-time job to earn that amount? Applying for scholarships is work, too, there's just no guarantee there will be a payoff.

- Be realistic; there are hundreds of applicants for many of these scholarships. You can't assume that your student will be awarded enough scholarships to cover all their costs. The so-called "full-ride" scholarships are few and far between.

- Scholarship timetables don't always mesh with decision-making time. Other than scholarships offered by the colleges your student is considering, you may not know if your student has been awarded some of the scholarships he or she applied for until after your student has decided which college to attend.

Looking for scholarships is a big, time-consuming effort. The best and easiest place to start is with scholarships offered at your student's prospective schools by checking the school's website or financial aid office. There are also several free scholarship search resources available. The U.S. Department of Labor has a free scholarship search engine on its website (http://careerinfonet.org/scholarshipsearch/ScholarshipCategory.asp?searchtype=category&nodeid=22). Sites like scholarship.com and fastweb.com also offer comprehensive listings of various scholarships available. You can also reach out to the state agency listed in the previous State-Based Aid section and ask about state scholarships. If your child already has a major in mind, it would be helpful to research professional organizations associated with that field and determine if there are any scholarships available to college students.

Another great resource in your search for scholarships is your guidance counselor—again (see why it's so important to have a strong, collaborative relationship with this person?). Guidance counselors can help alert you to local, state, and regional scholarships—the ones given by a service group in your community, or offered by a state foundation, or from a corporation in the area. They get lots of information about these types of scholarships that may not be publicized on national websites. And because they're local and drawing from a smaller potential pool of applicants, your student has a better chance at earning them. Your local news media or public library may also have information on scholarships in your area.

I also recommend that you buy *The "C" Student's Guide to Scholarships* by Felecia Hatcher. Here's why it's such a great resource: the author won over $130,000 in scholarships and had a GPA under 3.0, so she certainly knows what she's talking about and will inspire your student. I didn't do nearly that well, but I did receive a few scholarships, so here is an overview of some of the types of scholarships available.

Traditional: Traditional scholarships are either merit-based or need-based. Merit-based means that your student earned the GPA, test score, class rank, or other academic achievement necessary to qualify for the scholarship. Need-based means that the scholarship is awarded based on the student's socioeconomic status. For need-based scholarships, you will probably have to submit tax information and/or other documentation (such as your FAFSA) to prove need.

Most colleges have their own traditional scholarships available, both merit- and need-based. In many cases, a student's qualifying information for these scholarships is submitted automatically when he or she applies for admission to the school, but check to be sure that an additional application or step isn't necessary. In the case of most colleges' individual scholarships, the earlier you apply, the better—once the funds for a given year are allocated to incoming students, that's it.

In addition, there are hundreds of other traditional scholarship programs available, ranging from big national programs, like the Gates Millennium Scholarship Fund to local programs in your community. All have varying qualifications, requirements, and deadlines. Each will have its own application form and may also require grade transcripts, an essay, and/or letters of recommendation. Some traditional scholarships may have additional qualifications for applicants, such as gender, race, nationality, or students who are the first in their families to attend college.

Talent: Talent-based scholarships run the gamut and are not necessarily tied to academics. Does your student have any talents that can be capitalized on in the scholarship search? Of course, athletic scholarships are the first that come to mind here, but only Division I and Division II schools can offer those, and the competition is very tough. Does your daughter dance? Is your son in the band? Even programs they participated in during high school may have some scholarships available. So be sure to investigate whether something your child loves could provide some college money for your family.

Essays: There are lots of essay-based scholarship competitions. If your child loves to write, have them go at it! The awards can range from $500 to tens of thousands of dollars. Your student will be doing a lot of writing in college—why not start now?

Area of Study: If your student knows what he or she is going to major in, there are often scholarships for students pursuing degrees in certain subject areas. Keep in mind that some of them aren't available until after your student enrolls in school and declares a major, but it is still worth investigating.

Your Own Connections: Check with your employer about any available scholarships for the children of employees. You should also check with groups that you are a part of, such as fraternal organizations, service clubs, veterans groups, and so on. Many regional and national organizations that you may be part of have scholarships available for students.

Weird Scholarships: These are the outrageous ones that you hear about on the news, such as the scholarship for left-handed students or the one that gives college money to students who make their prom attire out of duct tape. The latest is a scholarship for kids whose parents met on Match.com! There are many wacky scholarship possibilities out there for things we never even think of, from doing duck calls to the National Candy Technologists Scholarship for students who may concoct the next great candy bar. Sure they're crazy, but somebody's got to win them, right? If your student happens to meet these unusual qualifications, they might as well go for it!

Check out Peterson's *Scholarships, Grants & Prizes* guide for trustworthy information on sources of private aid that may be able to help you lower the cost of your student's college education. The book offers detailed profiles on awards based on residence, military service, religious affiliation, talents or interest area, nationality or ethnic heritage, and employment/volunteer experience—and much more!

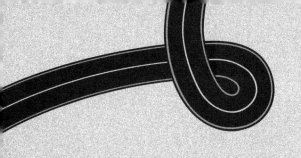

CHAPTER 7

Summer: An Important Part of Your Student's College Plan

Hooray, it's summertime! While your student may have dreams of sleeping late, spending time with friends, and having fun, you may need to step in with some alternative plans. Not that there isn't a time and a place for fun and relaxation, but it's important not to let eight to twelve weeks pass by with little or nothing to show for it. Your student needs to do something, so here are some suggestions.

Volunteer Work: Real-World Perspective and a Great Résumé Boost

Although it may seem difficult to find the time to have your student volunteer, the benefits he or she will draw from the experience will create a lifetime of memories and can be worth more than what your student would make working at a job during the summer. Your child could volunteer abroad or in your own community. The possibilities are endless.

There are a number of volunteer programs that allow your student to volunteer abroad.

- Global Leadership Adventures (GLA) (www.experiencegla. com) has great summer volunteer options abroad for high school students. GLA offers different themes: children's issues, environment and ecology, sports, poverty alleviation, public health, traditional culture, animals and wildlife, language learning, and leadership activities.

- The ISV High School Program (www.isvolunteers.org/destination/costa-rica/high-school-programs) offers an 18-day volunteer experience in Costa Rica.
- VISIONS Service Adventures (https://visionsserviceadventures.com) offers Spanish, French, and English language-immersion volunteer experiences for both high school and middle school students.

These are just a few of the possible volunteer-abroad programs; an online search will likely turn up dozens more.

Your student doesn't have to travel abroad to volunteer. Look for a food pantry in your community and find out if the organizers allow high school students to volunteer. Your child could assist with sorting donations and distributing goods. There may also be soup kitchens that need volunteers to assist on the serving line. Local libraries often offer reading programs for younger students. Your son, for example, could help a younger child learn how to read or read books to a group of children, thus reinforcing his own reading skills. Do some research into what is offered in your area, and I am sure you will find an opportunity that fits your child's personality and interests. It's often easier for students to find hours for volunteering in summer instead of trying to squeeze it in during the school year. Your student may be able to create a combination of volunteer work and a few hours at a part-time job, too.

Academic Options to Build a Solid Foundation

Starting with your child's first summer in high school, summer school can be a great idea, particularly if you want your student to get ahead in core classes and work on weaknesses. For example, students with challenges in math can use the summer to get ahead in their math track by taking a class that prepares them for honors or advanced-level courses. There are also intensive math courses that span several weeks of the summer. Or students can also use the summers to take composition or creative writing courses to strengthen their writing skills. Check to see what kinds of summer school programs are available in your school district, ask your student's guidance counselor for other options, or do some searching on your own.

In addition to addressing weaknesses, you might want to consider a program designed to build upon your student's strengths. For example, if your daughter is interested in technology, try a program that teaches high school students how to design their own mobile apps, such as Georgia Tech's summer program for high school students (http://coe.gatech.edu/content/high-school-programs).

Many colleges offer summer academic programs for high school students. Here are just a few options:

- Columbia University has a summer program that provides students with a taste of college life in a highly supervised setting. This program gives them an opportunity to learn from college professors, and it allows students to obtain a statement of attendance and evaluations from Columbia professors that they can use for other opportunities.

- Awesome Math (https://www.awesomemath.org/summer-program) offers a summer camp at the University of Texas at Dallas, Cornell University, and the University of California, Berkeley.

- Alfred University (http://www.alfred.edu/summer/camps/writing.cfm) offers a creative writing camp for rising sophomores, which covers poetry, short fiction, drama, and more.

There are hundreds of these kinds of summer programs—and many are probably offered at colleges close to your home. Whether it's a few days, a few weeks, or even two months, any program that puts your student on a college campus and gives them a taste of what college could be like is a valuable experience that can help them envision their future: walking between buildings, eating in a campus dining facility, staying in the dormitories, and taking classes in rooms that are equipped differently than their high school classrooms. It helps whet their appetite for what lies ahead and gives them a greater understanding of what it will be like to go to school away from home. Spending a little time on a college campus now can help students know what they want—and don't want—as they tour colleges in the years ahead, and it will keep them motivated toward their ultimate goal after graduation.

If your student is nervous about the start of their college career, you may want to look into summer programs at numerous colleges that help ease the transition into college life. These programs usually allow students to stay on campus, take advantage of an on-campus meal plan, and take one or two entry-level college courses. Keep in mind that these programs are usually at larger colleges and universities and may have a substantial cost associated with them. What may be more economically feasible is for your student to take one or two classes at a local community college. These classes are generally less expensive, more preparatory in nature, and can certainly help your student get ready for his or her rigorous freshman year studies.

Major-Related Programs

By the time students reach the end of tenth grade, they might have an idea of what major they'd like to study in college. Summer programs related to those fields could be a good opportunity to explore and learn more about different fields. They could come away with additional knowledge about professions and a stronger desire to pursue them, or they might learn that it's not the right major for them. Either way, it's a valuable lesson!

For example, students who are artistically inclined may want to try Northwestern University's National High School Institutes (http://nhsi.northwestern.edu) where students who excel in theater, film, or debate can hone their talents through intensive workshops in their areas of interest. The University of Southern California's Summer Seminars (http://summer.usc.edu/index.shtml) offer two- and four-week programs on more than twenty topics ranging from architecture to global health to graphic design. These are just a few examples—with a little searching online, you may be able to find something in your state or region that pertains to your student's interests.

What if you can't find a college-based program like this that's accessible to your student—either financially or geographically? Take a look at what's happening in your town or nearby city. For example, in Philadelphia, WHYY-TV, the PBS station, offers "student-centered learning experiences," such as film and journalism summer camps, for those in grades 6–12, giving students real hands-on learning and enabling them to see what's really involved in putting news stories and documentaries together.

Another possibility is to try to arrange a job-shadowing opportunity by reaching out to local professionals who are doing the job your child would like to someday do. Could your budding attorney spend a day or two in a law office, watching what goes on, or sitting in a courtroom, seeing that actual trial proceedings look a lot different than they do on TV? Or would it be possible for your student who is thinking about becoming a construction engineer to spend a day on a job site, watching firsthand all that is involved? The contacts your child makes early on could possibly lead to an internship if he or she eventually pursues that profession in college.

Internships

The summer after eleventh grade is a good time for your student to seek an internship in a profession he or she is considering. For example, if your daughter says she wants to become a reporter, she might want to apply for an internship at a local newspaper or the news department of a local radio or television station. Chances are she won't get paid, but she'll have an opportunity to see what the job really entails (as opposed to what she thinks it does!), and she'll be able to determine if she really does want to pursue a career in journalism.

Students interested in finding internships should seek out local small companies or offices in their field of interest. The smaller the company, the more willing management might be to take on a high school summer intern. Large companies often tend to only recruit college summer interns.

A Google search of "summer high school internships" will pull up myriad potential opportunities, including some possible dream internships with the U.S. Environmental Protection Agency (EPA) and the Goddard Space Center, as well as those in the fashion, business, medical, and engineering fields. Be sure to note the application requirements and deadlines for all summer internships.

In addition, don't forget to use your networking skills. Encourage your student to reach out to your friends, neighbors, and family members who may be working in that particular field. And, as I've recommended numerous times in this book, have your student check with their guidance counselor for any possible connections with high school alumni in the area for a potential summer internship.

Study-Abroad Programs: A Great Way to Improve Language Skills

The summer after tenth grade or eleventh grade might be a good time to consider a program abroad. While a student might be able to see a lot of sights on a ten-day tour, if your student is truly seeking to improve their foreign language skills, remember that true cultural immersion will usually take more than a month. To improve speaking skills in the foreign language your child is studying in school, it's obviously most helpful to travel to a country where that language is spoken. In order to make the most of the experience, students should try to stay away from programs with too many other Americans, and try to devote themselves to one place for the entire stay.

For example, if your student is taking Spanish in school, it might be better to go to Mexico or a Central American country in the summer rather than Spain, which is often teeming with American tourists then. If, however, your daughter, who is studying French, has an opportunity to travel with a group of U.S. students to France, encourage her to avoid speaking English the entire time with her friends and, instead, speak French—even if it's a struggle—as much as possible with the shopkeepers, and so on. It seems like the obvious thing to do, but it takes courage to move out of your comfort zone and speak the language of the country you're visiting.

Summer study-abroad programs provide an amazing opportunity for high school students to get a taste for international travel. Being fortunate enough to spend one's summer months in another culture can be a life-changing experience. It's not only an incredible way to learn a new language, but it also enables a student to explore an entirely new part of the world. And, depending on the summer program, it may even be possible to earn valuable credits toward college.

There are benefits to any sort of travel abroad, even if it isn't language-based or isn't long enough to provide cultural immersion. A tour of several European countries offers exposure to history, art, and culture that can't be replicated in a textbook or classroom. Any visit beyond our borders provides lessons in geography, government, and sociology. It's important that students—tomorrow's global citizens—become comfortable and confident travelers, able to adapt and function outside of their normal environment.

Worried about the cost? Many summer study-abroad programs offer need-based scholarships and financial aid. It's definitely worth exploring the many possibilities.

Domestic Travel and Family Vacations

Valuable summer travel opportunities don't have to include a passport. There's plenty to be learned within the United States that will stimulate and educate your entire family—and seem like fun, too. Whether you load up the minivan for a two-week trek along the East

Coast or can only squeeze in a weekend at a nearby historic site, it can still provide great lessons and special family memories (made all the more poignant by knowing that your student will be leaving home in a year or two).

It doesn't take much to look at popular tourist destinations with an eye toward education. Don't just drive by—instead, try to learn along the way. There's history to be found in every state. Tours of manufacturing plants offer exposure to business and industry; even passing miles of cropland and herds of cattle offer exposure to a discussion of agricultural and environmental issues. Explore geology at Yellowstone National Park, marine biology along the ocean shore, botany in the redwood forests, or astronomy when you venture beyond the city limits. It might be a stretch, but there are even physics and engineering lessons to be had at a theme park. Keep in mind that museums today aren't what they used to be when you were younger. Staffs at museums have worked hard to shed the old reputation as dark, boring places. Instead, today's museums engage the senses and inform all ages in unique ways—so don't pass them up on your summer travels. There is no shortage of opportunities for hands-on, interactive, in-person learning during the summer.

Many faith-based organizations offer mission trips or work camps, where youth travel to another location to provide service to others in need, often repairing homes or providing tutoring or services for younger children. These aren't vacations—these trips are often to impoverished areas, and students may sleep on the floor in a church basement—but they can be eye-opening experiences that boost your student's maturity, provide direction, build character, and give your child a newfound appreciation for their own home and education.

For some students, the summer YMCA or Scout camp they loved when they were younger may still be a place where they'd like to return as a counselor for an opportunity of growth and reflection.

Oh, and if that road trip to the family reunion takes you past a major college or university, consider planning ahead and scheduling a brief tour if time permits, or even spend a little time driving around the campus and looking at the facilities. It reinforces the "I'm-going-to-college" mindset and makes an impression on younger siblings, too. Every destination offers something to be learned there and along the way!

Athletic Programs

If your child plays a sport in high school and plans to continue in college, summer is a great time to continue with conditioning and training. Many colleges offer summer camps that allow high school students to boost their athletic skills with college coaches as well as professional sports players to give them an idea of the level of play necessary to successfully compete at the college level.

For example, for over ten years, the Detroit Lions Summer Youth Football Camps has been offering football training for students—from beginners to advanced-level players. In addition to its touted "high-energy" instruction, scrimmages, chalk talk, and video analysis, the summer program also provides students life lessons and leadership seminars, which are fantastic takeaways from any summer program.

No matter what sport your child is interested in or has been playing throughout their academic career, there are likely numerous summer programs taking place on high school or college campuses from which they can benefit. If your son or daughter currently plays a sport, I recommend that you reach out to their coach to discuss potential opportunities in your area.

Summer Employment—Earn Some Bucks and More!

Summer employment is a great option for any summer. First, it teaches responsibility and helps prepare your child for the real world. Furthermore, it can help your family offset some of the costs associated with preparing to send your child away to school.

A part-time or full-time summer job carries more benefits than just a paycheck. Students develop a work ethic and learn accountability, commitment, how to take direction, people skills, and the satisfaction of a job well done. And it's something else to add to that all-important college resume.

College books are expensive, plain and simple. Money earned during the summers can help pay for those books, as well as the numerous other items that your student will no doubt need during their first semester—and the ones to follow. Encouraging your student to work, especially during the summer after senior year, can help your child take ownership of his or her college education—and the financing of it—by being an active participant in the process from day one.

Some Help in This Book to Get You Started

As you begin to research potential summer programs for your student, check the Appendix: Resources for some useful online links. As always, I encourage you to reach out to your child's guidance counselor as a reference as well. Your counselor will know what programs are available in your area and can refer you to programs and/or jobs based on your child's interests.

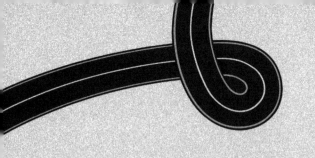

APPENDIX

Resources

COLLEGE BOUND

Financial Fundamentals

Saving For College
(www.savingforcollege.com/529_plan_details)

The 529 program is a great resource that is used by millions of parents each year. Plan details for each state are available online. This website is a good place to start investigating what 529 options are available to you.

Upromise® *(www.upromise.com)*

Upromise® is a corporation owned by Sallie Mae (the Student Loan Marketing Association) that helps you earn as you spend, much like a credit card rewards program. To participate, you create a Upromise account, then with every purchase at participating grocery or drug stores, restaurants, local retailers, or online stores, you can earn money that can later be used toward college tuition. Just keep in mind that it takes a lot of spending over a good many years to be able to apply these funds toward a large portion of a student's college education.

The SAGE Scholars Tuition Rewards® Program
(www.tuitionrewards.com)

The SAGE Scholars Tuition Rewards® Program (TRP) is a privately administered college savings program that rewards investment dollars with scholarship "points" that can be used at more than 320 colleges nationwide. The list of participating schools is available on this website.

Free Application for Federal Student Aid (FAFSA) *can be found on this website: fafsa.ed.gov.*

FAFSA Downloadable Guide *(http://www.studentaid.ed.gov/ sites/default/files/2014-15-completing-fafsa.pdf)*

FAFSA on the Web Worksheet *(http://studentaid.ed.gov/sites/ default/files/2014-15-fafsa-worksheet.pdf)*

FAFSA Deadlines at a Glance
(http://www.fafsa.ed.gov/deadlines.htm)

Enter your state to find your financial aid deadlines here.

FAFSA IRS Data Retrieval Tool
(https://fafsa.ed.gov/help/irshlp9.htm)

Rather than having to input all of your tax information into the FAFSA system, this site provides a tool that allows you to automatically import your tax information from the IRS.

CSS/Financial Aid PROFILE®
(http://student.collegeboard.org/css-financial-aid-profile)

In addition to the FAFSA, some schools (usually private colleges) require the CSS/Financial Aid PROFILE® through the College Board. The PROFILE is an online application that collects information used by those colleges and certain scholarship programs to award financial aid. You can build your child's CSS PROFILE on this site.

State-Based Aid *(http://wdcrobcolp01.ed.gov/Programs/EROD/ org_list.cfm?category_ID=SHE)*

Most states offer some sort of aid to students who are residents of their state and plan to attend college in their state. The U.S. Department of Education website has a State Education Agency Directory, which provides the contact information for the appropriate agency in your state. You can find this directory on the above site.

Scholarship Search Engine *(http://careerinfonet. org/scholarshipsearch/ScholarshipCategory. asp?searchtype=category&nodeid=22)*

The U.S. Department of Labor has created a free scholarship search engine. You can filter and access hundreds of scholarships through this site.

Scholarship Search *(www.scholarship.com)*

This website allows your child to search for, find, and apply for scholarships online.

Fastweb *(www.fastweb.com)*

This website allows your student to search for scholarships online and even delivers them to your inbox daily.

Getting Organized

Asana *(www.asana.com)*

If you love checklists as much as I do, you will love Asana—it's the best shared checklist ever. If you create a task in Asana, you can assign it to your student with a due date. Asana will remind you both via e-mail when the task is due or if it becomes past due.

Basic Calendar Creator *(http://www.timeanddate.com/calendar/basic.html)*

This page allows you to create a basic customized calendar for keeping track of your student's deadlines and other key dates.

College Application Wizard *(http://collegeappwizard.com/)*

The College Application Wizard is a great tool that claims to be most personalized, comprehensive, streamlined, and anxiety-reducing way to navigate college admission and financial aid applications. This tool does everything we have discussed with respect to checklists and organizing for you. It will remind you what to do and when to do it. To reduce future headaches, this may be worth checking out—and yes, it's free.

College Application Checklist *(https://bigfuture.collegeboard. org/get-in/applying-101/college-application-checklist)*

The College Board application checklist is simple and easy to use.

Campus Explorer (*https://www.campusexplorer.com/ registration/planner/?backref=%2Fmyplanner%2F)*

This site offers an interactive checklist. It also provides access to college searches, scholarships, financial aid tips, and more.

My College Calendar *(http://www.mycollegecalendar.org/ explore/pdf/application-checklist-pdf.pdf)*

This website provides a college application checklist and calendar.

Toodledo *(http://www.toodledo.com/)*

This is a to-do list on steroids with a hotlist, customizable alarms, and a sortable online to-do list to help you remember to complete tasks on time. It's available for your mobile phone, in your e-mail, on your calendar, integrated directly into your web browser, and more.

Majors and Careers

Education Planner *(Educationplanner.org)*

On this website, your student can learn about various careers as well as colleges. There are interactive exercises, with to-the-point instructions to help your child prepare for important decisions like choosing a major. This site is a public service of the Pennsylvania Higher Education Assistance Agency, FedLoan Servicing, and American Education Services.

Jung Typology Test
(www.humanmetrics.com/cgi-win/JungType.htm)

This is similar to the Myers-Briggs Type indicator. It helps to define your student's personality type formula, and it offers a career indicator test, which suggests possible career choices based on that personality type.

Keirsey Temperament Sorter
(www.keirsey.com/sorter/register.aspx)

This can be a good indicator of your student's likes and dislikes, which can then lead you to explore careers that fit his or her personality type.

The MAPP™ Career Assessment Test *(www.assessment.com)*

This website indicates that more than 7 million people have taken the 15-minute MAPP career test—that's a lot of people. You can get a sample report and five possible career matches for free, but there is a cost for additional information. However, it may be worth it given the reports and analysis the test report provides.

Personality Test for High School Students *(www.high-school. devry.edu/personality-profile/questions.htm)*

This website offers career guides specific to high school students. It offers growth statistics for particular fields of study and offers an online personality profile with recommendations for various personality types.

U.S. Bureau of Labor Statistics *(http://www.bls.gov/ooh/)*

The Occupational Outlook Handbook lets you browse and check out information on hundreds of occupations.

Standardized Testing and Test-Prep Information

ACT *(www.actstudent.org)*

Find ACT test dates and locations, register, prep for the test, interpret your scores—it's all here. This is the company that writes and administers the ACT; therefore, materials cover only that test.

ACT College Readiness Report *(http://www.act.org/readinessreality/13/index.html)*

The ACT College Readiness Report is a body of research compiled by the drafters of the ACT exam that analyzes the state of college readiness of high school students who took the exam for the current year. The report discusses whether or not the students are, on average, prepared for college course work based on their ACT test scores. The results are broken down by grade as well as by demographics.

Bell Curves (*www.bellcurves.com*)

I have to mention Bell Curves because I wish this company could be everywhere. The Bello brothers are test-prep snobs, but in a totally great way. Hashim Bello came to Atlanta to teach a group of aspiring law students how to take the LSAT and was honestly one of the best instructors I've seen. Bell Curves' teachers truly care about their students, about how their students learn, and about how they teach. They will figure out how to make your student get it. If you are in New York City, you should enroll your student in one of these courses. Note, however, that Bell Curves only offers prep courses for the SAT.

BenchPrep (*benchprep.com*)

BenchPrep is a test-prep buffet. This company provides everything on your student's computer, iPad, or any other device for a reasonable monthly fee. BenchPrep has acquired the resources of hundreds of providers to give students options and access, anytime and anywhere, to put the power of online learning in your child's hands.

College Board (*www.collegeboard.org*)

Here's where you need to go to register, prepare, and get scores for the SAT and PSAT/NMSQT tests. This is the company that writes and administers the SAT; therefore, materials cover only that test.

eKnowledge Corporation (*www.eknowledge.com/Affiliate_ Welcome.asp?coupon=3A8E9CEFCE*)

If you are in the military or are a veteran, eKnowledge offers free test-prep courses for your child. The courses are delivered via online videos, books, and DVDs.

FreeTestPrep.com (*www.freetestprep.com*)

Freetestprep.com provides help through practice tests, online guides, and flashcards. The guides are in the form of a blog that discusses various topics related to test prep. For example, one article is a test-anxiety guide. It covers the roots of test anxiety and provides students with tips to combat their anxiety. The flashcards section covers ACT/SAT math formulas, SAT vocabulary words, SAT writing and grammar, and ACT English and grammar. The flashcards are by far the most valuable resources on this site.

Kaplan (*www.kaptest.com*)

This is the big guy in test prep. There's nothing wrong with being a big guy, but be careful when enrolling your student in a big guys' course. They are hit or miss. If your child doesn't need much one-on-one attention and truly only needs to get an overview, this may be the right class for him or her.

Number2.com *(www.number2.com)*

Number2.com claims to be the only website that offers students access to comprehensive and free online test-preparation courses for the SAT®, ACT®, and GRE®. I have had my students use the site to access the free practice tests. The vocabulary builder section is particularly useful to bolster your student's verbal skills for the SAT. What I find particularly useful about this resource is that you can keep track of how much work your child has completed and verify their work through the website. Just be sure to create your own account, and add your child as a student under your profile.

The Princeton Review *(www.princetonreview.com)*

This is another one of the big guys. The great thing about the big-guy courses is that your child will have access to tons and tons of practice questions, and that's great. You have to remember that both of the big guys on this list are international companies that enroll hundreds of thousands of students each year. It seems impossible to enroll that many students and provide everyone with all the attention they need, so the big guys generally offer money-back guarantees, or, at a minimum, allow your student to retake the course.

Revolution Prep *(www.revolutionprep.com)*

Revolution Prep provides live and online courses. This company is unique because it is committed to community as much as to test prep. The company has a generous scholarship program, company service days, and partnership programs to help students in the community. It has also worked to embrace technology in its test-prep strategies by using it to create a personalized online learning environment.

SAT® Redesign Information
(www.collegeboard.org/delivering-opportunity/sat/redesign)

Major changes are being made in the SAT test. If your child is planning to take the SAT after March 2016, he or she needs to be aware of these changes. Visit this website for more information on how the SAT is changing.

SparkNotes *(www.sparknotes.com/testprep)*

SparkNotes is a cheat sheet for standardized tests, books, and more. The creators of this site have a knack for breaking things down into easy-to-understand instructions. SparkNotes tells about each test and how best to study for it. The site doesn't provide actual, live practice tests; however, its test-prep books are available for purchase.

Top Test Prep *(toptestprep.com)*

Top Test Prep is a high-end educational services company. Since the company uses the phrase "high-end" in describing itself and fails to list a price for its services on the website, the price may be pretty high.

VeritasPrep *(www.veritasprep.com)*

The founder of VeritasPrep scored a perfect score on the SAT, and the company is staffed with instructors who not only scored extremely high on the SAT but also attended Ivy League schools.

Summer Programs

[Author's note: This is just a very small sampling of the myriad opportunities throughout the country for high school students. Remember to also check out the summer courses or programs for high school students at your local colleges and universities that offer your student exceptional enrichment for the summer.]

Alfred University
(http://www.alfred.edu/summer/camps/writing.cfm)

This university offers a creative writing camp for rising high school sophomores, which covers poetry, short fiction, drama, and more.

Awesome Math
(https://www.awesomemath.org/summer-program)

This company offers a summer camp at the University of Texas at Dallas, Cornell University, and the University of California, Berkeley.

Columbia University Summer Program
(http://ce.columbia.edu/high-school)

Columbia University has a summer program that provides students with a taste of college life in a highly supervised setting. This program gives them an opportunity to learn from college professors, and it allows students to obtain a statement of attendance and evaluations from Columbia professors that they can use for other opportunities.

Cornell University Summer College
(http://www.sce.cornell.edu/sc/)

Cornell University offers precollege programs that enable high school students to experience college life. Students can take courses with Cornell faculty members in 3-week or 6-week summer sessions.

Global Leadership Adventures *(www.experiencegla.com)*

This company has great summer volunteer options abroad for high school students. It offers different themes: children's issues, environment and ecology, sports, poverty alleviation, public health, traditional culture, animals and wildlife, language learning, and leadership activities.

ISV (International Student Volunteers) High School Program *(www.isvolunteers.org/destination/costa-rica/high-school-programs)*

Students can participate in a new 18-day volunteer/travel experience in Costa Rica, where they will volunteer for about 80 hours helping with community development initiatives, teaching children, or assisting with a sea turtle conservation program.

Lifeworks International *(http://lifeworks-international.com)*

Lifeworks International offers summer programs and camps for teens. During trips to locations throughout the world, high school students experience adventure travel, cultural immersion, community service, and global education.

Northwestern University's National High School Institutes *(http://nhsi.northwestern.edu)*

Northwestern University offers a program where students who excel in theater, film, or debate can hone their talents through intensive workshops in their areas of interest.

Penn Summer High School Programs *(http://www.sas.upenn.edu/summer/programs/highschool)*

Here at the University of Pennsylvania, students can get a taste of college life at an Ivy League institution. Academically intensive, noncredit programs are offered in such topics as biomedical research, chemistry research, experimental physics, and social justice research. Residential and commuter options are available.

Summer Programs at Johns Hopkins University
(http://pages.jh.edu/summer/precollege/index.html)

High school students can take undergraduate classes in a wide variety of topics in the "Summer University" at Johns Hopkins University and get a taste of college life at the same time. The "Discover Hopkins Programs" offer unique courses for commuter and residential students in the health studies field.

The University of Southern California's Summer Seminars
(http://summer.usc.edu/index.shtml)

University of Southern California offers both two- and four-week programs on more than twenty topics ranging from architecture to global health to graphic design.

VISIONS Service Adventures
(https://visionsserviceadventures.com)

VISIONS Service Adventures offers Spanish, French, and English language-immersion volunteer experiences for both high school and middle school students.

Supplemental Learning Programs

AP Course Offerings
(https://apstudent.collegeboard.org/exploreap)

This website will provide you with detailed information on current AP courses. This is a general list of potential courses and does not mean that these courses are offered at your student's school.

Figure This! *(figurethis.org)*

This site, which offers fun math challenges for students and their families, is a great way for middle- and/or high-school students to review the basics. The website was created by the National Council of Teachers of Mathematics, in cooperation with the National Action Council for Minorities in Engineering, Widmeyer Communications, and the Learning First Alliance, with funding from the National Science Foundation and the U.S. Department of Education.

HippoCampus (*hippocampus.org*)

This is a free, core academic website that delivers rich multimedia content—videos, animations, and simulations—on general education subjects to middle- and high-school teachers and college professors, and their students.

Khan Academy *(www.khanacademy.org)*

Students can make use of this extensive library of content, including interactive challenges, assessments, and videos from any computer with access to the web. A student can begin at the basics and work gradually into calculus or jump right into whatever topic needs some brushing up.

The Longman Vocabulary Website
(http://wps.ablongman.com/long_licklider_vocabulary_2/)

Here, your student will find exercises that cover a wide range of vocabulary-related topics: word parts, dictionary exercises, context clues, synonyms, antonyms, homonyms, and more.

Math Planet *(www.mathplanet.com)*

This site's goal is to spread mathematical knowledge worldwide. Everything on the site is free to use, and you don't need to register in order to watch the videos or read examples.

Math Forum *(mathforum.org)*

A leading online resource for improving math learning, teaching, and communication since 1992, this website was developed by the Drexel University School of Education so that teachers, mathematicians, researchers, students, and parents could use the power of the Web to learn math and improve math education.

Powerspeak K12 *(www.power-glide.com)*

The K12 offering in foreign languages helps students read, write, speak, and listen for meaning in any of five target languages: Spanish, French, German, Latin, and Chinese. Unlike many second-language programs that are recycled adult-learning products, powerspeaK12 is designed specifically for students in grades 3 through 12.

Spelling City *(www.spellingcity.com)*

This is an award-winning, game-based learning tool for vocabulary, spelling, writing, and language arts. The program is also available as a downloadable app.

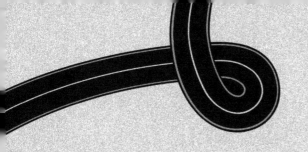

A Final Thought

COLLEGE BOUND

A FINAL THOUGHT

Any student who gets into college does not do so by accident. It takes a well-coordinated plan and strategy to earn admission to college. As a proactive parent, you are willing to do what it takes to improve your child's educational opportunities, and I hope this book has helped take some of the mystery out of college readiness for you. Thank you for reading, and I wish you and your high school student much success.

—Amber C. Saunders, Esq.